Company's Coming®

150 DELICIOUS SQUARES

by
Jean Paré

Dedication

Special thanks to my mother, Ruby Elford, from whom I learned to appreciate good cooking. Also dedicated to my father, Edward Elford, who praised even my earliest attempts.

Cover Photo

1. Caramel Slice page 65
2. Lemon Slice page 48
3. Cherry Triangles page 77
4. Butter Tart Bars page 140
5. Neapolitan Squares page 83
6. Chocolate Cherry Slice page 64

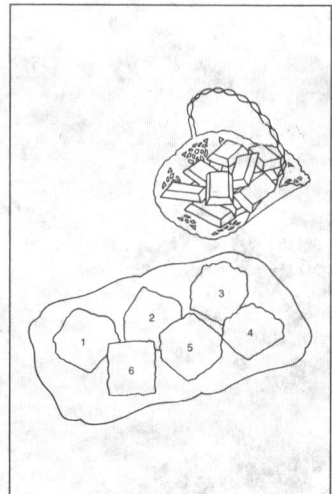

Silver Creamer And Tray Courtesy Of:
The Bay China Dept.

Tablecloth Courtesy Of:
Special Event Rentals

150 DELICIOUS SQUARES

Copyright © 1981 by Company's Coming Publishing Limited
All Rights Reserved
Revised 1995 Edition

Thirty-fourth Printing July 1996

ISBN 0-9690695-0-2

Published and Distributed by
Company's Coming Publishing Limited
Box 8037, Station "F"
Edmonton, Alberta, Canada
T6H 4N9

**Published Simultaneously in
Canada and the United States of America**

Printed In Canada

Company's Coming Cookbooks by Jean Paré

COMPANY'S COMING SERIES
English

- 150 DELICIOUS SQUARES
- CASSEROLES
- MUFFINS & MORE
- SALADS
- APPETIZERS
- DESSERTS
- SOUPS & SANDWICHES
- HOLIDAY ENTERTAINING
- COOKIES
- VEGETABLES
- MAIN COURSES
- PASTA
- CAKES
- BARBECUES
- DINNERS OF THE WORLD
- LUNCHES
- PIES
- LIGHT RECIPES
- MICROWAVE COOKING
- PRESERVES
- LIGHT CASSEROLES
- CHICKEN, ETC.
- KIDS COOKING
- FISH & SEAFOOD
- BREADS
- MEATLESS COOKING (April 1997)

PINT SIZE BOOKS
English

- FINGER FOOD
- PARTY PLANNING
- BUFFETS
- BAKING DELIGHTS
- CHOCOLATE

JEAN PARÉ LIVRES DE CUISINE
French

- 150 DÉLICIEUX CARRÉS
- LES CASSEROLES
- MUFFINS ET PLUS
- LES DÎNERS
- LES BARBECUES
- LES TARTES
- DÉLICES DES FÊTES
- RECETTES LÉGÈRES
- LES SALADES
- LA CUISSON AU MICRO-ONDES
- LES PÂTES
- LES CONSERVES
- LES CASSEROLES LÉGÈRES
- POULET, ETC.
- LA CUISINE POUR LES ENFANTS
- POISSONS ET FRUITS DE MER
- LES PAINS
- LA CUISINE SANS VIANDE (avril 1997)

table of Contents

The Jean Paré Story 6

Foreword 7

Unbaked Squares 8

Baked Squares 46

Measurement Tables 152

Index 153

Mail Order Form 157

the Jean Paré story

Jean Paré grew up understanding that the combination of family, friends and home cooking is the essence of a good life. From her mother she learned to appreciate good cooking, while her father praised even her earliest attempts. When she left home she took with her many acquired family recipes, her love of cooking and her intriguing desire to read recipe books like novels!

In 1963, when her four children had all reached school age, Jean volunteered to cater to the 50th anniversary of the Vermilion School of Agriculture, now Lakeland College. Working out of her home, Jean prepared a dinner for over 1000 people which launched a flourishing catering operation that continued for over eighteen years. During that time she was provided with countless opportunities to test new ideas with immediate feedback—resulting in empty plates and contented customers! Whether preparing cocktail sandwiches for a house party or serving a hot meal for 1500 people, Jean Paré earned a reputation for good food, courteous service and reasonable prices.

"Why don't you write a cookbook?" Time and again, as requests for her recipes mounted, Jean was asked that question. Jean's response was to team up with her son, Grant Lovig, in the fall of 1980 to form Company's Coming Publishing Limited. April 14, 1981, marked the debut of "150 DELICIOUS SQUARES", the first Company's Coming cookbook in what soon would become Canada's most popular cookbook series. By 1995, sales had surpassed ten million cookbooks.

Jean Paré's operation has grown from the early days of working out of a spare bedroom in her home to operating a large and fully equipped test kitchen in Vermilion, Alberta, near the home she and her husband Larry built. Full-time staff has grown steadily to include marketing personnel located in major cities across Canada plus selected U.S. markets. Home Office is located in Edmonton, Alberta where distribution, accounting and administration functions are headquartered in the company's own 20,000 square foot facility. Growth continues with the recent addition of the Recipe Factory, a 2700 square foot test kitchen and photography studio located in Edmonton.

Company's Coming cookbooks are now distributed throughout Canada and the United States plus numerous overseas markets, all under the guidance of Jean's daughter, Gail Lovig. The series is published in English and French, plus a Spanish language edition is available in Mexico. Soon the familiar and trusted Company's Coming style of recipes will be available in a variety of formats in addition to the bestselling soft cover series.

Jean Paré's approach to cooking has always called for quick and easy recipes using everyday ingredients. She continues to gain new supporters by adhering to what she calls "the golden rule of cooking": never share a recipe you wouldn't use yourself. It's an approach that works—*ten million times over!*

Foreword

For almost as long as I can remember, I have been compiling recipes in boxes, scrap books, files and more boxes. Through years of catering, I have used most of the recipes in this book at one function or another, many of which have been requested by those attending.

The first step in being able to cut perfect squares is to line the pan with foil. Once the squares have been thoroughly chilled or baked and cooled, you can remove them from the pan. Simply lift them out by holding the edges of the foil and place them on a cutting surface. For a 9 x 9 inch (22 x 22 cm) pan, use a long, sharp knife to cut the square in half. Be sure to clean the knife between every cut. Press straight down through the center of each half, and cut in half again. Working on one quarter at a time, cut each section into three strips. Then turn and make three cuts the other way. Each section yields nine squares, making a total of 36 for the whole pan. An 8 x 8 inch (20 x 20 cm) pan may be cut into 36 squares if it is a rich recipe. Otherwise, you may have to use a ruler to cut 5 by 5 pieces to make 25.

To cut through a top chocolate layer, heat the knife in hot water. Dry it quickly with a paper towel and press down slowly so the chocolate softens slightly as you make the cut. Clean the knife in hot water and repeat for each cut.

Every recipe in this book has been tried and taste-tested many times. You may freeze each recipe very successfully, except where stated otherwise. However, for best results, I recommend icing the squares one or two days before serving. All the icings can be made and frozen in separate containers. Be sure to allow icing to reach room temperature before using. If more liquid is needed, it may be added then. When added before room temperature is reached, icing will be runny when it warms. Accompanying photographs will help you to visualize your choice of squares before baking.

Make some squares. Brew some coffee. Call your friends. Company's coming!

Jean Paré

CHOCOLATE ROLL

This is a colorful confection. It freezes well. After a few slices are cut, you can pop it back in the refrigerator or freezer. The icing sugar gives it a very smooth texture.

Semisweet chocolate chips	1 cup	250 mL
Butter or hard margarine	2 tbsp.	30 mL
Large egg, beaten	1	1
Icing (confectioner's) sugar	1 cup	250 mL
Miniature colored marshmallows	2½ cups	625 mL
Quartered maraschino cherries, well drained	½ cup	125 mL
Chopped walnuts	½ cup	125 mL
Medium coconut, for coating		

Melt chocolate chips and butter in large heavy saucepan over low heat. Stir often. Remove from heat.

Add egg, icing sugar, marshmallows, cherries and walnuts. Stir to mix. Cool if very warm. Form mixture into a roll.

Sprinkle some coconut over countertop, in space big enough to move roll around to coat with coconut. After well-coated, wrap in either waxed paper or plastic wrap. Chill before slicing. Slice thinly with sharp knife. Clean knife in hot water after cutting each slice.

Pictured on page 17.

The best time to sample all the goodies you want is when you are so tired or so busy that you will forget you had any. Your body can't remember if your brain forgets.

PEANUT BUTTER RICE KRISPIES

I think this was intended for the kids but we all eat and enjoy them.

Sweetened condensed milk	⅔ cup	150 mL
Smooth peanut butter	¼ cup	60 mL
Corn syrup, light or dark	¼ cup	60 mL
Brown sugar, packed	½ cup	125 mL
Crisp rice cereal	4 cups	1 L
ICING		
Semisweet chocolate chips	½ cup	125 mL
Smooth peanut butter	2 tbsp.	30 mL

Heat first 4 ingredients in large saucepan, stirring constantly, until well mixed and thickened. Remove from heat.

Add rice cereal, stirring to coat. Pack into greased 9 x 9 inch (22 x 22 cm) pan. Cool.

Icing: Melt chocolate chips and peanut butter over low heat, stirring often. Spread over squares. Cuts into 36 squares.

Pictured on page 17.

RICE KRISPIES

Is there a child that doesn't ask for these again and again?

Butter or hard margarine	¼ cup	60 mL
Large marshmallows	32	32
Crisp rice cereal	5 cups	1.25 L

Melt butter in large heavy saucepan.

Add marshmallows and stir over low heat until they are melted.

Add rice cereal. Stir until well-coated. Press into buttered 8 x 8 inch (20 x 20 cm) pan or 9 x 9 inch (22 x 22 cm) pan. Let stand for a few hours to set before cutting. Cuts into 25 or 36 squares.

Pictured on page 53.

Variation: Melt 3 tbsp. (50 mL) butter or hard margarine and 1 cup (250 mL) semisweet chocolate chips over low heat, stirring often. Spread over top.

CHOCOLATE CRISPS

Any age can make this in a flash. It is like candy to eat.

Honey	¾ cup	175 mL
Smooth peanut butter	1 cup	250 mL
Semisweet chocolate chips	1 cup	250 mL
Salted peanuts	1 cup	250 mL
Crisp rice cereal	3 cups	750 mL

Melt honey and peanut butter in a large saucepan over low heat. Bring slowly to a boil. Remove from heat.

Add chocolate chips. Stir until melted.

Add peanuts and rice cereal. Stir to coat. Press into greased 9 x 9 inch (22 x 22 cm) pan. Chill well before cutting. Cuts into 25 or 36 squares.

Pictured on page 53.

S'MORES

These can be made as fast as they can be eaten. Great for picnics around a campfire. Mmmm, s'more please!

Whole graham crackers
Thin milk chocolate bars
Large marshmallows

Each S'More square will need 2 crackers. A large cracker will need 4 squares of chocolate to fit nicely. Put chocolate on cracker. Put marshmallow on fork and toast over fire or red-hot burner. When toasted and melting, push on top of chocolate. Cover with second cracker, pressing down. Wait for 1 or 2 minutes before eating so that the chocolate begins to melt from heat of marshmallow. Another method is to put cracker, chocolate and marshmallow under broiler; then cover with second cracker when done.

Pictured on page 53.

Variation: Use chocolate mint wafers (such as After-Eight Mints) instead of chocolate bars.

FANCY WHIP UP

A pretty confection. Very easy.

Whole graham crackers

Butter or hard margarine, softened	½ cup	125 mL
Icing (confectioner's) sugar	1½ cups	375 mL
Large egg	1	1
Salt, sprinkle		
Vanilla	¾ tsp.	4 mL
Medium coconut	1 cup	250 mL
Chopped maraschino cherries, well-drained	½ cup	125 mL
Chopped walnuts	½ cup	125 mL

Whole graham crackers

ICING

Icing (confectioner's) sugar	1½ cups	375 mL
Butter or hard margarine, softened	3 tbsp.	50 mL
Vanilla	½ tsp.	2 mL
Water	1½ tbsp.	25 mL

Line ungreased 8 x 8 inch (20 x 20 cm) pan with crackers, trimming to fit.

Beat butter, icing sugar and egg until light.

Add salt, vanilla, coconut, cherries and walnuts. Mix well. Spread over crackers in pan. Smooth top.

Cover with second layer of graham crackers.

Icing: Beat all 4 ingredients together in bowl. Add more liquid or icing sugar to make icing the proper consistency. Spread over top. Let stand a few hours, covered, to allow crackers to soften. Store in refrigerator. Cuts into 25 squares.

Pictured on page 17.

BABA RUM ROLL

You can make this more or less rummy by adjusting the water measurement.

Vanilla wafer crumbs (11 oz., 300 g)	3 cups	750 mL
Cocoa	3 tbsp.	50 mL
Apricot jam, sieved	4 tbsp.	60 mL
Rum (see Note)	3 tbsp.	50 mL
Water (see Note)	2-3 tbsp.	30-50 mL
Apricot jam, sieved	1 tbsp.	15 mL
Water	2 tsp.	10 mL

Chocolate sprinkles, for coating

Combine wafer crumbs with cocoa in medium bowl. Stir in first amount of jam and rum. Add water adjusting to a little more or a little less. If crumbs are very fine it can make a difference. Squish well until it will hold together. Shape into 1 or 2 logs.

Combine second amounts of jam and water. Coat logs well with this mixture.

Roll in chocolate sprinkles to coat well. Do not cover at this point or it will get very wet and runny. Allow to dry and then wrap. Slice in thin slices as needed.

Note: If not using rum, combine 2 tsp. (10 mL) rum flavoring and water to measure 5 to 6 tbsp. (75 to 100 mL).

Pictured on page 17.

COCONUT ROLL

A slice with few ingredients. For coconut lovers.

Fine coconut	1½ **cups**	375 mL
Smooth peanut butter	½ **cup**	125 mL
Corn syrup, light or dark	2 tbsp.	30 mL

Fine coconut, to coat

Mix first amount of coconut, peanut butter and corn syrup well until dampened. Add a bit more syrup if it won't cling together when worked well. Form into roll.

Roll in more coconut to coat well. Wrap and store in refrigerator. Cut in thin slices to serve.

Pictured on page 17.

MIDNIGHT MINTS

The perfect ending to lunch or supper. The minty taste goes with just about anything.

BOTTOM LAYER
Butter or hard margarine	½ cup	125 mL
Granulated sugar	¼ cup	60 mL
Cocoa	⅓ cup	75 mL
Large egg, beaten	1	1
Graham cracker crumbs	1¾ cups	425 mL
Finely chopped walnuts	½ cup	125 mL
Fine coconut	¾ cup	175 mL

SECOND LAYER
Butter or hard margarine, softened	⅓ cup	75 mL
Milk	3 tbsp.	50 mL
Peppermint flavoring	1 tsp.	5 mL
Icing (confectioner's) sugar	2 cups	500 mL
Green food coloring		

TOP LAYER
Semisweet chocolate chips (see Note)	⅔ cup	150 mL
Butter or hard margarine	2 tbsp.	30 mL

Bottom Layer: Combine butter, sugar and cocoa in saucepan. Bring slowly to a boil. Stir in egg to thicken. Remove from heat.

Stir in graham crumbs, walnuts and coconut. Work together well. Pack very firmly into greased 9 x 9 inch (22 x 22 cm) pan.

Second Layer: Combine butter, milk, flavoring and icing sugar in bowl. Beat together well adding a bit more milk if needed to make spreadable. Tint a pretty green. Spread over first layer.

Top Layer: Melt chocolate chips and butter in saucepan over low heat or hot water. Stir often. Cool. When cool but still runny, spread over second layer. Chill and store, covered, in refrigerator or freezer. Cuts into 36 squares.

Pictured on page 53.

Note: You may also use 4 x 1 oz. (4 x 28 g) semisweet chocolate baking squares.

OH HENRY BUTTERSCOTCH

You will find, of all the no-bake bars, this is a favorite. Be sure to try this one.

Whole graham crackers

Butter or hard margarine	¾ cup	175 mL
Brown sugar, packed	⅔ cup	150 mL
Milk	½ cup	125 mL
Vanilla	1 tsp.	5 mL
Graham cracker crumbs	1¼ cups	300 mL

Whole graham crackers

ICING

Icing (confectioner's) sugar	1½ cups	375 mL
Butter or hard margarine, softened	3 tbsp.	50 mL
Water	4 tsp.	20 mL
Vanilla	½ tsp.	2 mL

Line ungreased 9 x 9 inch (22 x 22 cm) pan with graham crackers, trimming to fit.

Combine butter, brown sugar, milk and vanilla in large saucepan. Bring to a boil and simmer for 5 minutes. Remove from heat.

Stir in graham crumbs. Pour over crackers in pan.

Cover with layer of crackers, trimming to fit. Cool.

Icing: Beat all 4 ingredients together in small bowl. Add more water if icing seems too stiff to spread or more icing sugar if it is too runny. Spread over top. Cuts into 36 squares.

Pictured on page 17.

CEREAL SLICE

The name of this should be changed because it doesn't taste anything like breakfast. You don't need the oven for this one.

Corn syrup, light or dark	½ cup	125 mL
Brown sugar, packed	½ cup	125 mL
Smooth peanut butter	½ cup	125 mL
Corn flakes	2 cups	500 mL
Crisp rice cereal	1 cup	250 mL
ICING		
Brown sugar, packed	½ cup	125 mL
Cream (or milk)	2 tbsp.	30 mL
Butter or hard margarine	¼ cup	60 mL
Icing (confectioner's) sugar	1 cup	250 mL

Heat corn syrup and brown sugar in saucepan, stirring until sugar is dissolved. Remove from heat. Stir in peanut butter until smooth.

Add corn flakes and rice cereal. Stir to coat well. Press in greased 9 x 9 inch (22 x 22 cm) pan. Spread in 8 x 8 inch (20 x 20 cm) pan for a smaller but thicker product.

Icing: Measure brown sugar, cream and butter into saucepan. Bring to a boil and allow to boil for 1 minute. Cool.

Add icing sugar. Beat with spoon, adding more icing sugar or cream if necessary to get proper spreading consistency. Spread over top. Cuts into 36 squares.

Pictured on page 17.

While attending a convention, this is your chance to consume all kinds of extras. After all, it is a professional obligation, not food intake.

FLAT TRUFFLES

A snap to make. A smooth creamy texture that melts in your mouth.

Butter or hard margarine, softened	½ cup	125 mL
Cocoa	⅓ cup	75 mL
Icing (confectioner's) sugar	¾ cup	175 mL

Crushed walnuts or pecans, for coating

Cream butter until soft and pliable. Sift in cocoa to ensure there are no lumps. Blend well. Add icing sugar, sifting if there are any lumps. Mix well, adding more icing sugar if too soft to roll. You will be able to work 1 or 2 spoonfuls at least into batter. Shape into roll.

Roll in walnuts. Chill for several hours. Serve in slices.

Pictured on page 17.

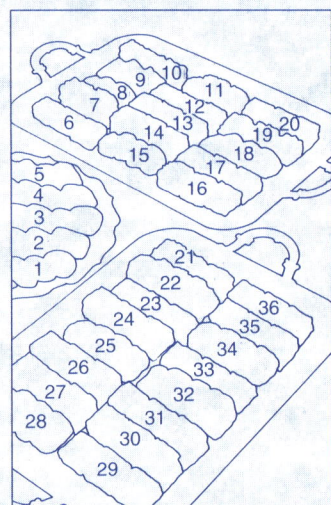

1. Baba Rum Roll page 12
2. TV Roll page 32
3. Marshmallow Roll page 38
4. Chocolate TV Roll page 28
5. Graham Mint Roll page 19
6. Cereal Slice page 15
7. Nummies page 37
8. Fruit Roll page 20
9. Rainbow Pastel page 25
10. Millionaire Squares page 45
11. Pineapple Log page 39
12. Butterscotch Coconut Squares page 27
13. Raisin Quickie page 22
14. Tropical Treat page 29
15. Flat Truffles page 16
16. Cherry Wonder page 30
17. Peanut Butter Rice Krispies page 9
18. Coconut Roll page 12
19. Butterscotch Confetti page 33
20. Krispy Krunch Bars page 38
21. Chow Mein Noodles page 34
22. Bridge Peel Dainties page 24
23. Nanaimo Bars page 40
24. Festive Fruit page 43
25. Snow Log page 24
26. Chocolate Carousels page 31
27. Fudgy Macaroons page 20
28. Chocolate Cherry Creams page 33
29. Chocolate Boil page 21
30. Fancy Whip Up page 11
31. Chocolate Coconut Layer page 25
32. Chocolate Roll page 8
33. Chocolate Peanut Squares page 32
34. Apricot Roll page 19
35. Oh Henry Butterscotch page 14
36. Saucepan Brownies page 23

Silver Trays Courtesy Of:
Special Event Rentals

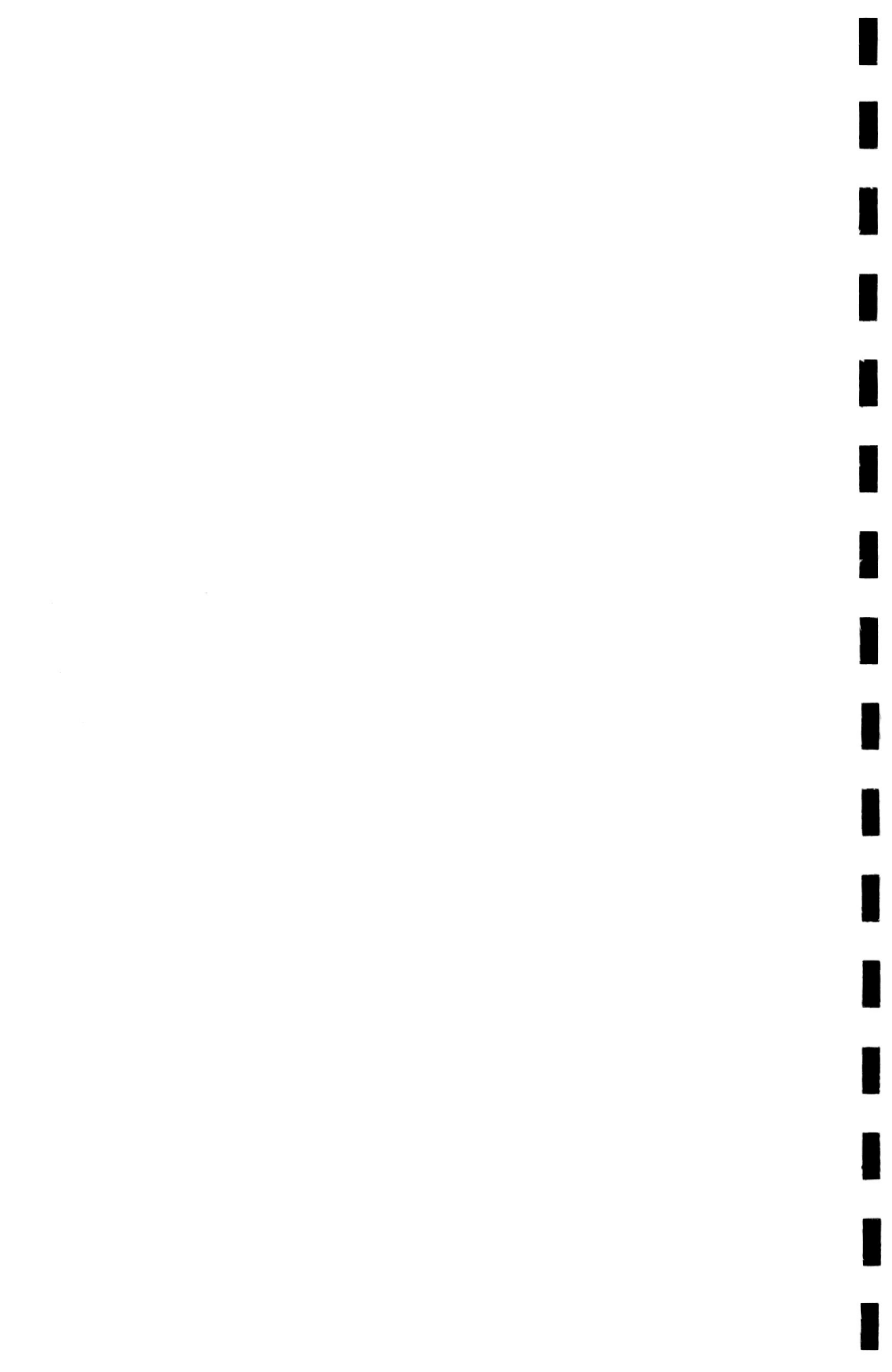

GRAHAM MINT ROLL

These can be shaped into tiny rolls to serve as an after-lunch mint substitute.

Graham cracker crumbs	2 cups	450 mL
Tiny after-dinner mints	1 cup	250 mL
Sweetened condensed milk	11 oz.	300 mL
Medium coconut	½ cup	125 mL

Medium coconut, for coating

Place graham crumbs in medium bowl. Grind mints in food processor or grinder and add to crumbs. Stir in condensed milk and first amount of coconut. Let stand for 5 or 10 minutes in bowl.

Sprinkle second amount of coconut on waxed paper. Put mixture over top and shape into 2 logs. Roll in coconut until coated. Chill in plastic wrap. Slice as needed.

Pictured on page 17.

APRICOT ROLL

Not as sweet as most rolls.

Chopped dried apricots	1 cup	250 mL
Chopped dates	½ cup	125 mL
Vanilla wafer crumbs	¾ cup	175 mL
Grated lemon rind	2 tsp.	10 mL
Medium coconut	½ cup	125 mL
Icing (confectioner's) sugar	⅓ cup	75 mL
Brandy flavoring	2 tsp.	10 mL
Prepared orange juice	3 tbsp.	50 mL

Granulated sugar

Combine apricots and dates in bowl along with wafer crumbs, lemon rind, coconut and icing sugar.

Mix brandy flavoring with orange juice, then add to fruit mixture. Form into roll, adding a bit more orange juice if needed.

Roll in sugar. Chill in refrigerator. Slice thinly, as required.

Pictured on page 17.

FUDGY MACAROONS

Crunchy butterscotch treats. Similar taste to brown sugar fudge.

Evaporated milk	1 cup	250 mL
Granulated sugar	1½ cups	375 mL
Butter or hard margarine	¼ cup	60 mL
Vanilla	1 tsp.	5 mL
Butterscotch chips	2 cups	500 mL
Corn flakes, pushed down slightly in cup	4 cups	1 L
Medium coconut	2½ cups	625 mL
Chopped walnuts	1 cup	250 mL

Combine evaporated milk, sugar and butter in saucepan. Bring to a full rolling boil over medium heat. Remove from heat.

Add vanilla and butterscotch chips. Stir until chips are melted.

Stir in corn flakes, coconut and walnuts. Spread in greased or foil-lined 9 x 9 inch (20 x 20 cm) pan. Chill well before cutting. Cuts into 36 squares.

Pictured on page 17.

FRUIT ROLL

The sweetness of this roll comes mostly from the fruit.

Chopped dates	½ cup	125 mL
Chopped candied cherries	½ cup	125 mL
Chopped candied pineapple	¼ cup	60 mL
Raisins	½ cup	125 mL
Chopped walnuts	¼ cup	60 mL
Salt	⅛ tsp.	0.5 mL
Medium coconut	¼ cup	60 mL
Granulated sugar, to coat		

Put first 7 ingredients through a food chopper or processor. Mix well, adding a bit of water if needed to make it cling together. Form into log 2 inches (5 cm) in diameter.

Roll in granulated sugar. Chill. Cut into thin slices, as needed.

Pictured on page 17.

CHOCOLATE BOIL

Here is another of those time-saver, no-bake, medium-sweet squares.

Butter or hard margarine	½ cup	125 mL
Cocoa	2 tbsp.	30 mL
Milk	1 tbsp.	15 mL
Brown sugar, packed	1 cup	250 mL
Large eggs, beaten	2	2
Graham cracker crumbs	3 cups	700 mL
Medium coconut	½ cup	125 mL
Chopped walnuts	½ cup	125 mL
Salt	¼ tsp.	1 mL
ICING		
Semisweet chocolate chips	1 cup	250 mL
Butter or hard margarine	2 tbsp.	30 mL

Bring butter, cocoa, milk, sugar and eggs to a boil in saucepan, stirring often. Boil 1 minute.

Stir in next 4 ingredients. Press into greased (or foil-lined) 9 x 9 inch (22 x 22 cm) pan. Cool.

Icing: Melt chocolate chips and butter in saucepan over low heat, stirring often. Spread over cooled bars. Allow to set before cutting. Store in refrigerator. Cuts into 36 squares.

Pictured on page 17.

A friend has gone to a lot of work to serve you a deliciously rich lunch. It simply doesn't count, no matter what kind of a diet you are on. That is good manners, not a meal.

RAISIN QUICKIE

One saucepan does it all. Rich caramel taste.

Whole graham crackers

Raisins	¾ cup	175 mL
Water	¼ cup	60 mL
Butter or hard margarine	½ cup	125 mL
Cocoa	1 tbsp.	15 mL
Granulated sugar	1 cup	250 mL
Large egg, beaten	1	1
Graham cracker crumbs	1 cup	250 mL
Chopped walnuts	½ cup	125 mL

Whole graham crackers, to cover

ICING

Icing (confectioner's) sugar	1¼ cups	300 mL
Cocoa	¼ cup	60 mL
Butter or hard margarine, softened	3 tbsp.	50 mL
Water or prepared coffee	1½ tbsp.	25 mL

Line ungreased 9 x 9 inch (22 x 22 cm) pan with graham crackers, trimming to fit.

Boil raisins and water for 2 minutes in large saucepan.

Reduce heat. Add butter, cocoa, sugar and egg. Stir to combine until butter melts and mixture thickens slightly. Remove from heat.

Add graham crumbs and walnuts. Stir. Pour over graham crackers in pan.

Cover with layer of graham crackers, trimming to fit.

Icing: Beat all 4 ingredients together in bowl, adding more water if needed to make icing soft enough to spread. Spread over top layer of graham crackers. Store, covered, in refrigerator. Cuts into 36 squares.

Pictured on page 17.

SAUCEPAN BROWNIES

At last, a brownie that you can make on a day which is too hot to think about food. It has an exceptionally rich chocolate flavor.

Semisweet chocolate chips	2²⁄₃ cups	650 mL
Evaporated milk	1 cup	250 mL
Vanilla wafer crumbs	3 cups	750 mL
Miniature marshmallows	2 cups	500 mL
Chopped walnuts	1 cup	250 mL
Icing (confectioner's) sugar	1 cup	250 mL
Salt	½ tsp.	2 mL
Evaporated milk	2 tsp.	10 mL
Reserved chocolate mixture	½ cup	125 mL

Put chocolate chips and first amount of evaporated milk in large saucepan. Melt over medium-low heat, stirring often, until smooth. Remove from heat. Measure out ½ cup (125 mL) and reserve for final step.

Stir wafer crumbs, marshmallows, walnuts, icing sugar and salt into remaining chocolate mixture in saucepan. Press in greased or foil-lined 9 x 9 inch (22 x 22 cm) pan.

Stir second amount of evaporated milk into the reserved chocolate mixture. Spread evenly over brownies. Chill. Cuts into 36 squares.

Pictured on page 17.

A good time to eat is when you are daydreaming. If you eat without thinking about it, it can't count against you.

SNOW LOG

A cherry-flavored slice. Light in color which makes it a good contrast for a tray of sweets.

Cream cheese, softened	4 oz.	125 g
Icing (confectioner's) sugar	1½ cups	375 mL
Vanilla wafer crumbs	1¼ cups	300 mL
Salt	¼ tsp.	1 mL
Chopped maraschino cherries, well-drained	½ cup	125 mL

Vanilla wafer crumbs, for coating

Beat cream cheese until smooth. Beat in icing sugar. Mix in first amount of wafer crumbs, salt and cherries. You may have to add more icing sugar. You can safely add as much as you can work in. Shape into a log 1½ to 2 inches (4 to 5 cm) in diameter.

Roll in wafer crumbs to coat. Store in waxed paper in a plastic bag. Keep in refrigerator. Cut in thin slices to serve.

Pictured on page 17.

BRIDGE PEEL DAINTIES

You can't guess the taste of these by looking at them — you have to try them. Let them stand for a day or two before using if possible.

Cut mixed fruit peel	2 cups	500 mL
Chopped dates	1 cup	250 mL
Chopped walnuts	1 cup	250 mL
Sweetened condensed milk	11 oz.	300 mL
Miniature marshmallows	2 cups	500 mL
Graham cracker crumbs	1½ cups	350 mL

Graham cracker crumbs, to coat

Combine first 6 ingredients in bowl. Mix until evenly coated. Shape into 2 logs.

Roll in graham crumbs. Wrap in waxed paper and store in plastic bag in refrigerator. Cut in thin slices when needed.

Pictured on page 17.

CHOCOLATE COCONUT LAYER

This makes a good contrast using the light and dark layers. Chocolate really adds to it.

Icing (confectioner's) sugar	5¼ cups	1.2 L
Medium coconut	3¾ cups	850 mL
Vanilla	¾ tsp.	4 mL
Egg whites (large), slightly beaten	3	3
Butter or hard margarine	¾ cup	175 mL
Cocoa	2 tbsp.	30 mL

Mix icing sugar, coconut, vanilla and egg whites in mixing bowl.

Melt butter and allow to cool before adding to first mixture. Spread ½ of batter in greased 8 × 8 inch (20 × 20 cm) pan. Smooth top. Cool.

Add cocoa to the remaining ½ of batter. After stirring well, press second ½ over first layer. Chill. Cuts into 25 squares.

Pictured on page 17.

RAINBOW PASTEL

Those who love coconut will appreciate these colorful squares. They are simple to make and add variety to a tray of goodies.

Sweetened condensed milk	11 oz.	300 mL
Icing (confectioner's) sugar	2 cups	500 mL
Fine coconut	1 lb.	454 g

Red, yellow and green food coloring

Combine condensed milk, icing sugar and coconut in bowl. Stir to mix. Divide into 3 equal portions.

Tint 1 portion a delicate pink, 1 yellow and the other green. Pack in ungreased small loaf pan, 1 layer at a time. Start with pink, then yellow, then green. Refrigerate and cut as needed. To freeze, wrap airtight to keep from drying.

Pictured on page 17.

PUFFED WHEAT SQUARES

One of the best child-pleasers going.

Butter or hard margarine	¼ cup	60 mL
Corn syrup, light or dark	⅓ cup	75 mL
Brown sugar, packed	½ cup	125 mL
Cocoa	1½ tbsp.	25 mL
Puffed wheat	6 cups	1.5 L

Combine butter, corn syrup, sugar and cocoa in saucepan. Stir over medium heat until it begins to bubble. Boil 1½ minutes. Remove from heat.

Pour over puffed wheat in bowl. Stir until all puffed wheat is coated. Press firmly in greased 8 x 8 inch (20 x 20 cm) pan. Cool. Let stand awhile before cutting. Cuts into 25 squares.

Pictured on page 53.

JELLIED MARSHMALLOWS

A tricky little number that will bring "How did you do that?" from everyone.

Any flavored gelatin (jelly powder)	3 oz.	85 g
Boiling water	⅔ cup	150 mL
Granulated sugar	1 cup	250 mL
Light corn syrup	3 tbsp.	50 mL
Icing (confectioner's) sugar, to coat		

Put jelly powder and boiling water into small saucepan on low heat. Stir to dissolve. Add granulated sugar stirring to dissolve. Mix in corn syrup. Turn into bowl. Cool. Place rubber spatula in bowl and refrigerate. Set timer for 10 minutes. Stir, scraping down sides of bowl. Continue to set timer for 10 minute intervals, stirring and scraping sides down each time. It should get almost as stiff as liquid honey but you don't want it to get chunky. Beat for 5 minutes or until stiff. Pour into 8 x 8 inch (20 x 20 cm) pan that has been lined with waxed paper. Chill overnight.

Sift some icing sugar over counter top or bread board. Turn jellied squares over onto icing sugar. Remove waxed paper by gently rubbing damp cloth over and letting stand for a few minutes. After all paper is off, dust with icing sugar. As each piece is cut, dust well all over with icing sugar. Cuts into 25 squares.

Pictured on page 53.

BUTTERSCOTCH COCONUT SQUARES

This doesn't require baking and is very tasty. For coconut lovers.

Butter or hard margarine	¼ cup	60 mL
Butterscotch chips	½ cup	125 mL
Vanilla	1 tsp.	5 mL
Large egg, slightly beaten	1	1
Salt	¼ tsp.	1 mL
Medium coconut	1 cup	225 mL
Chopped walnuts	½ cup	125 mL
Graham cracker crumbs	2 cups	450 mL
ICING		
Butter or hard margarine, softened	2 tbsp.	30 mL
Icing (confectioner's) sugar	1 cup	250 mL
Vanilla custard powder	1 tbsp.	15 mL
Vanilla	½ tsp.	2 mL
Milk	4 tsp.	20 mL

Melt butter and butterscotch chips over low heat, stirring often. Remove from heat.

Add next 6 ingredients. Stir well. Pack into greased 9 x 9 inch (22 x 22 cm) pan. Cool.

Icing: Blend all ingredients together adding a bit more icing sugar or milk if needed for proper spreading consistency. Spread over bottom layer. Chill well, covered, for several hours in refrigerator. Cuts into 36 squares.

Pictured on page 17.

Variation: Substitute semisweet chocolate chips for butterscotch chips.

CHOCOLATE CONFETTI

Much can be said about this square. So simple to make, children love it, adults love it, it keeps well and freezes for months. Adds color to a tray of goodies as well.

Butter or hard margarine	¼ cup	60 mL
Smooth peanut butter	½ cup	125 mL
Semisweet chocolate chips	1 cup	250 mL
Miniature colored marshmallows	8 oz.	250 g

Melt butter with peanut butter in a large saucepan. Stir in chocolate chips until melted. Cool so that you can hold your hand on the bottom of the pan.

Add marshmallows and stir until all are coated. Pack in 9 x 9 inch (22 x 22 cm) pan that has been lined with foil for easy removal to cut or freeze. Refrigerate. Cuts into 36 squares.

Pictured on page 53.

Variation: To above ingredients add ½ cup (125 mL) chopped walnuts and/or ½ cup (125 mL) medium coconut.

CHOCOLATE TV ROLL

This is a variation of the chocolate roll. It has cocoa instead of chips, and graham cracker crumbs which give a more grainy texture.

Large egg, beaten	1	1
Icing (confectioner's) sugar	1 cup	225 mL
Graham cracker crumbs	½ cup	125 mL
Cocoa	½ cup	125 mL
Butter or hard margarine, melted	2 tbsp.	30 mL
Miniature colored marshmallows	2½ cups	575 mL
Chopped walnuts	½ cup	125 mL

Medium coconut, for coating

Mix first 7 ingredients together in bowl. It will seem dry at first but keep working it until it is all moistened. Shape into a roll.

Roll in coconut. Wrap in plastic. Chill. Cut into thin slices.

Pictured on page 17.

TROPICAL TREAT

Coffee flavors this square which is indeed a treat from the tropics.

Vanilla wafer crumbs	5½ cups	1.25 L
Granulated sugar	1 cup	250 mL
Butter or hard margarine	¾ cup	175 mL
Instant coffee granules	3½ tsp.	17 mL
Milk	¾ cup	175 mL
Rum (or less rum flavoring)	4 tsp.	20 mL
ICING		
Icing (confectioner's) sugar	1¼ cups	300 mL
Butter or hard margarine, softened	2 tbsp.	30 mL
Prepared coffee	4 tsp.	20 mL

Measure wafer crumbs into large bowl. Set aside.

In small saucepan combine sugar, butter, coffee granules and milk. Heat, stirring until butter is melted. Bring to boil and remove from heat.

Stir in rum. Pour over crumbs in bowl and stir until thoroughly moistened. At this point you can add more wafer crumbs if you feel mixture is too soft. This will firm up very little when chilled. Spread in greased 8 x 8 inch (20 x 20 cm) pan. Chill.

Icing: Beat all ingredients together well, adjusting liquid or icing sugar as needed to make a spreadable icing. Spread over bars. Allow to set. Cuts into 25 squares.

Pictured on page 17.

Eating children's leftover food doesn't count. That is being thrifty.

CHERRY WONDER

Aptly named since so many cannot decide what it is that gives that flavor.

Whole graham crackers		
Butter or hard margarine, softened	½ cup	125 mL
Icing (confectioner's) sugar	1 cup	250 mL
Egg yolk (large)	1	1
Mashed banana	½ cup	125 mL
Chopped maraschino cherries, well-drained	½ cup	125 mL
Chopped walnuts	½ cup	125 mL
Medium coconut	1 cup	250 mL
ICING		
Butter or hard margarine, softened	3 tbsp.	50 mL
Icing (confectioner's) sugar	2 cups	500 mL
Vanilla	½ tsp.	2 mL
Water or milk	4 tsp.	20 mL
Finely chopped walnuts	1-2 tbsp.	15-30 mL

Line bottom of ungreased 9 x 9 inch (22 x 22 cm) pan with whole graham crackers, trimming to fit.

Cream butter, icing sugar and egg yolk. Add banana, cherries, walnuts and coconut. This won't get much firmer when chilled so now is the time to add more icing sugar to firm it up if it is a bit too soft. Spread over graham crust. Chill.

Icing: Beat butter, icing sugar, vanilla and water together, adding icing sugar or liquid as needed to reach proper spreading consistency. Spread over well-chilled bars.

Sprinkle with very finely chopped walnuts. Cuts into 36 squares.

Pictured on page 17.

CHOCOLATE CAROUSELS

This has a peanut butter flavor and looks nice and fruity. While it is usually iced, it is a pretty square without any icing. No baking is required.

Smooth peanut butter	2 cups	500 mL
Icing (confectioner's) sugar	2 cups	500 mL
Butter or hard margarine, softened	2 tbsp.	30 mL
Salt	1/8 tsp.	0.5 mL
Chopped dates	1 cup	250 mL
Chopped maraschino cherries, well-drained	1 cup	250 mL
Chopped pecans or walnuts	1 cup	250 mL
ICING		
Semisweet chocolate baking squares, cut up (see Note)	4 × 1 oz.	4 × 28 g
Smooth peanut butter	2 tbsp.	30 mL

Combine peanut butter, icing sugar, butter and salt in large bowl. Cream together well. Mixture will be stiff.

Add dates, cherries and pecans. Stir until mixed. Press firmly in 8 × 8 inch (20 × 20 cm) pan that has been lined with foil.

Icing: Melt chocolate and peanut butter in heavy saucepan over low heat, stirring often. Spread over Carousels. Refrigerate. Cuts into 25 squares.

Pictured on page 17.

Note: You may also use ⅔ cup (150 mL) semisweet chocolate chips.

Be sure to fill up your plate to overflowing. Then if you use proper manners, namely leave a bit of food, you will already have had your share.

CHOCOLATE PEANUT SQUARES

What an aroma! So chocolaty.

Semisweet chocolate chips	1½ cups	375 mL
Smooth peanut butter	¾ cup	175 mL
Chopped dates	1⅓ cups	325 mL
Bran flakes (cereal)	3 cups	750 mL
Coconut, sprinkle		

Put chocolate chips and peanut butter into saucepan and stir to melt over low heat. Remove from heat.

Add dates and bran flakes. Stir until well coated. Press in 9 x 9 inch (22 x 22 cm) pan that has been lined with foil.

Sprinkle with coconut. Chill thoroughly before cutting. Cuts into 36 squares.

Pictured on page 17.

TV ROLL

Try this differently colored marshmallow roll.

Large egg, beaten	1	1
Brown sugar, packed	1 cup	250 mL
Graham cracker crumbs	½ cup	125 mL
Butter or hard margarine, melted	2 tbsp.	30 mL
Miniature colored marshmallows	2 cups	500 mL
Chopped walnuts	½ cup	125 mL
Colored thread coconut (see Note)		

Mix first 6 ingredients in order given. Squish and mix by hand. Work between wax paper or dip hands in cold water as you work to mix and shape into log.

Roll log in coconut. Wrap in waxed paper, folding in ends to hold shape. Freezes well. Cut in thin slices as needed.

Pictured on page 17.

Note: If you cannot buy colored thread coconut, put desired food coloring drops in container with lid. Add coconut. Shake or stir to distribute color.

BUTTERSCOTCH CONFETTI

This freezes well for so long. There is no excuse not to have it on hand. That is, if you keep it hidden.

Butter or hard margarine	¼ cup	60 mL
Smooth peanut butter	½ cup	125 mL
Butterscotch chips	1 cup	250 mL
Miniature colored marshmallows	8 oz.	250 g

Melt butter and peanut butter in a large saucepan over low heat. Stir in butterscotch chips until melted. Cool until you can hold your hand on bottom of pot. To speed process, stir while holding pan in cold water until cool enough.

Add marshmallows and stir until all are coated. Pack in 9 x 9 inch (22 x 22 cm) pan that has been lined with foil. Refrigerate. Cuts into 36 squares.

Pictured on page 17.

Variation: To above ingredients, add ½ cup (125 mL) chopped walnuts and/or ½ cup (125 mL) medium coconut.

CHOCOLATE CHERRY CREAMS

Like a candy. Creamy and mouth watering.

Semisweet chocolate chips	1 cup	250 mL
Evaporated milk	½ cup	125 mL
Icing (confectioner's) sugar	3 cups	750 mL
Chopped walnuts	½ cup	125 mL
Chopped maraschino cherries, well-drained	⅓ cup	75 mL

Medium coconut, for coating

Melt chocolate chips and evaporated milk together in saucepan over low heat, stirring often. Remove from heat.

Stir in icing sugar, walnuts and cherries. If quite soft, work in an additional 2 or 3 spoonfuls of icing sugar. Chill for at least 1 hour.

Shape into 2 logs about 1½ or 2 inches (4 or 5 cm) in diameter. Roll in coconut. Chill several hours before cutting into thin slices with a sharp knife.

Pictured on page 17.

CHOW MEIN NOODLES

You have had this as a drop cookie no doubt. It is less time-consuming to put in a pan to be cut. Handy to have in the freezer for kids' lunches.

Semisweet chocolate chips	1 cup	250 mL
Butterscotch chips	1 cup	250 mL
Canned chow mein noodles (see Note)	4 oz.	113 g
Chopped walnuts	1 cup	250 mL
Flake coconut	1 cup	250 mL

Put both kinds of chips in saucepan over low heat to melt. Stir often as they melt.

Mix noodles, walnuts and coconut in large bowl. Pour melted chips over and mix well. Spoon into foil-lined 8 × 8 inch (20 × 20 cm) pan. Chill to harden before cutting. These should be stored in the refrigerator as they tend to become too soft and sticky at room temperature. Cuts into 25 squares.

Note: You may use 1½ cups (375 mL) bulk chow mein noodles broken in short pieces.

Pictured on page 17.

1. Pineapple Brownies page 69
2. Chocolate Orange Drops page 96
3. Merry Fruit Bars page 97
4. Date Pecan Bars page 95
5. Fruit Cocktail Bars page 81
6. Potato Chip Bars page 106
7. Prune Chips page 98
8. Cream Cheese Brownies page 80
9. Cherry Almond Squares page 79
10. Raspberry Meringue page 142
11. Chocolate Fruit Squares page 99
12. Pineapple Filled Bars page 104

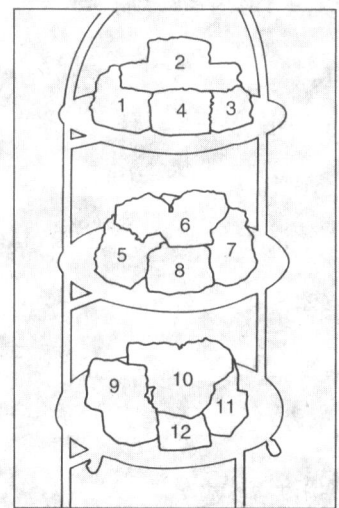

Plate Stand Courtesy Of:
Sears

Plates And Tray Courtesy Of:
Call The Kettle Black

NUMMIES

Not a sweet bar. The taste will win you over.

Graham crackers (about ½ box)	8 oz.	250 g
Miniature marshmallows	2½ cups	625 mL
Granulated sugar	½ cup	125 mL
Butter or hard margarine	½ cup	125 mL
Large egg, beaten	1	1
GLAZE		
Icing (confectioner's) sugar	1 cup	250 mL
Vanilla	½ tsp.	2 mL
Milk	1 tbsp.	15 mL

Break (be sure not to roll) graham crackers into pieces as you put them into large bowl. Add marshmallows. Set aside.

In top of double boiler or a heavy saucepan mix sugar, butter and egg. Cook and stir until syrupy. Pour over dry ingredients in bowl. Stir to coat evenly. Press in greased 8 x 8 inch (20 x 20 cm) pan.

Glaze: Mix all 3 ingredients in small bowl, adding enough milk so mixture will barely pour from spoon. Drizzle over top of bars. Let stand until firm. Cuts into 25 squares.

Pictured on page 17.

Keep talking while eating. The stomach doesn't know what is going on when the throat is so busy doing its own thing.

MARSHMALLOW ROLL

This is such a neat-looking sweet on any plate.

Unsweetened chocolate baking squares	2 × 1 oz.	2 × 28 g
Sweetened condensed milk	11 oz.	300 mL
Graham cracker crumbs	2 cups	450 mL
Finely chopped walnuts	½ cup	125 mL

Large colored marshmallows

Medium coconut, for coating

Melt chocolate in large saucepan over low heat or over hot water. Stir often. Remove from heat.

Stir in condensed milk, graham crumbs and walnuts. Divide into 2 portions.

On piece of waxed paper, press out 1 portion ¼ inch (0.5 cm) thick. Form into shape wide enough to go around marshmallow. Place various colors of marshmallows end to end and bring up batter to go around, pinching dough to join.

Coat with coconut. Repeat for other half. Wrap in waxed paper. Store in plastic wrap in refrigerator. Cut with knife dipped in hot water. Clean knife between cuts. Slice to serve.

Pictured on page 17.

KRISPY KRUNCH BARS

Little kids like these as much as big kids!

Smooth peanut butter	2 cups	500 mL
Icing (confectioner's) sugar	2½ cups	625 mL
Crisp rice cereal	2½ cups	625 mL
Butter or hard margarine, melted	¼ cup	60 mL
Chopped walnuts (optional)	½ cup	125 mL
ICING		
Semisweet chocolate chips	⅔ cup	150 mL
Butter or hard margarine	1 tbsp.	15 mL

(continued on next page)

Mix peanut butter, icing sugar, rice cereal, butter and walnuts in bowl. Press in 9 x 9 inch (22 x 22 cm) pan that has been lined with foil.

Icing: Melt chocolate chips and butter over low heat. Stir often. Spread over bars. Chill. Cuts into 36 squares.

Pictured on page 17.

PINEAPPLE LOG

A pretty little roll to have on hand. It keeps for ages in the freezer.

Cream cheese, softened	4 oz.	125 g
Icing (confectioner's) sugar	1 cup	250 mL
Vanilla wafer crumbs	3 cups	750 mL
Salt	¼ tsp.	1 mL
Crushed pineapple, drained	14 oz.	398 mL
Miniature colored marshmallows, cut in quarters (use scissors)	½ cup	125 mL
Colored thread coconut, for coating (see Note)		

Beat cream cheese until smooth. Add icing sugar, wafer crumbs, salt and pineapple. After mixing well, if this seems very soft, work more crumbs or icing sugar into the batter, keeping in mind that it won't get much firmer when chilled. The amount extra that you will need depends on how well you drained the pineapple.

Mix in marshmallows. Shape into 2 logs. Roll in coconut. Wrap and chill. Slice to serve.

Pictured on page 17.

Note: If you cannot buy colored thread coconut, put desired food coloring drops in container with lid. Add coconut. Shake or stir to distribute color.

NANAIMO BARS

A special occasion brings this to mind. You can make it the day before or even have it in the freezer.

BOTTOM LAYER
Butter or hard margarine	½ cup	125 mL
Granulated sugar	¼ cup	60 mL
Cocoa	⅓ cup	75 mL
Large egg, beaten	1	1
Graham cracker crumbs	1¾ cups	400 mL
Fine or medium coconut	¾ cup	175 mL
Walnuts, finely chopped	½ cup	125 mL

SECOND LAYER
Butter or hard margarine, softened	½ cup	125 mL
Milk	3 tbsp.	50 mL
Vanilla custard powder	2 tbsp.	30 mL
Icing (confectioner's) sugar	2 cups	500 mL

TOP LAYER
Semisweet chocolate chips (see Note)	⅔ cup	150 mL
Butter or hard margarine	2 tbsp.	30 mL

Bottom Layer: Melt first 3 ingredients in top of double boiler or in heavy saucepan.

Add beaten egg and stir to cook and thicken. Remove from heat.

Stir in graham crumbs, coconut and walnuts. Press firmly into ungreased 9 x 9 inch (22 x 22 cm) pan.

Second Layer: Cream butter, milk, custard powder and icing sugar together well. Beat until light. Spread over bottom layer.

Top Layer: Melt chocolate chips and butter over low heat. Cool. When cool but still runny, spread over second layer. Chill in refrigerator. Cuts into 36 squares.

Pictured on page 17.

Note: You may also use 4 x 1 oz. (4 x 28 g) semisweet chocolate baking squares.

PEANUT KRISPIE SQUARES

There is a chocolate frosting on this cereal cookie. It tastes as good as it looks.

Smooth peanut butter	½ cup	125 mL
Corn syrup, light or dark	½ cup	125 mL
Brown sugar, packed	½ cup	125 mL
Butter or hard margarine	4 tsp.	20 mL
Crisp rice cereal	2 cups	500 mL
Peanuts	1 cup	250 mL
ICING		
Butter or hard margarine	¼ cup	60 mL
Icing (confectioner's) sugar	½ cup	125 mL
Milk	3 tbsp.	50 mL
Vanilla	½ tsp.	2 mL
Icing (confectioner's) sugar	1½ cups	375 mL
Cocoa	2 tbsp.	30 mL

Heat the peanut butter, corn syrup, sugar and butter in a saucepan over low heat. Stir as you heat it.

Combine rice cereal and peanuts in bowl. Pour hot mixture over top. Stir well to coat evenly. Press in greased 8 x 8 inch (20 x 20 cm) pan.

Icing: Stir first 4 ingredients in saucepan until butter melts and it comes to a boil. Boil for 2 minutes. Cool to room temperature.

Add remaining icing sugar and cocoa. Mix well. Add a bit more milk or icing sugar if needed for proper spreading consistency. Spread over squares. Let stand to firm. Cuts into 25 squares.

Pictured on page 71.

CHOCOLATE OH HENRY SQUARES

You will find this top-of-the-stove square both fast and scrumptious. Keeps well. Freezes better uniced.

Whole graham crackers

Butter or hard margarine	¾ cup	175 mL
Brown sugar, packed	⅔ cup	150 mL
Milk	½ cup	125 mL
Semisweet chocolate chips	⅓ cup	75 mL
Graham cracker crumbs	1¼ cups	300 mL
Chopped walnuts	1 cup	250 mL

Whole graham crackers

ICING

Icing (confectioner's) sugar	1¼ cups	300 mL
Butter or hard margarine, softened	3 tbsp.	50 mL
Cocoa	¼ cup	60 mL
Hot prepared coffee	1½ tbsp.	25 mL

Line ungreased 9 x 9 inch (22 x 22 cm) pan with crackers, trimming to fit. Set aside.

Put butter, sugar and milk in saucepan. Bring to a boil.

Remove from heat and stir in chocolate chips. When chips have melted add the graham crumbs and walnuts. Stir to mix. Pour over crackers in pan.

Cover with whole graham crackers, trimming to fit. Cool.

Icing: Beat icing sugar, butter, cocoa and coffee together in small bowl, adjusting liquid or icing sugar as needed for proper spreading consistency. Spread over squares. Cover and allow to stand a few hours before cutting so the crackers will soften. Cuts into 36 squares.

Pictured on page 53.

FESTIVE FRUIT

This must be made two or three days before you attempt to cut it. Then you will consider it a real fruit cake.

Evaporated milk	⅔ cup	150 mL
Miniature marshmallows	2 cups	500 mL
Frozen concentrated orange juice	6 tbsp.	100 mL
Chopped dates	¾ cup	175 mL
Raisins	¾ cup	175 mL
Chopped walnuts	1 cup	250 mL
Cut mixed candied fruit	1 cup	250 mL
Chopped candied cherries	¼ cup	60 mL
Graham cracker crumbs	4 cups	900 mL
Ground cinnamon	1 tsp.	5 mL
Ground nutmeg	1 tsp.	5 mL
Ground cloves	½ tsp.	2 mL
ICING		
Icing (confectioner's) sugar	1½ cups	375 mL
Butter or hard margarine, softened	3 tbsp.	50 mL
Vanilla	½ tsp.	2 mL
Water or milk	1½ tbsp.	25 mL

Combine evaporated milk, marshmallows and orange juice in saucepan over medium heat. Stir until marshmallows are melted. Remove from heat.

Put dates, raisins, walnuts, fruit and cherries into large bowl. Pour melted mixture over and stir.

Add graham crumbs and spices. Mix well. Press in foil-lined 9 x 9 inch (22 x 22 cm) pan. Cover tightly. Chill 2 or 3 days.

Icing: Beat icing sugar, butter, vanilla and water together in small bowl adjusting liquid or icing sugar as needed for proper spreading consistency. Spread over fruit squares on day you intend to serve. Chill. Cuts into 36 squares.

Pictured on page 17.

OH HENRY BARS

A really scrumptious square. No need to use the oven. If you happen to be a little short of walnuts, coconut or cherries, you can vary the quantities without anyone knowing it wasn't meant to be that way.

Whole graham crackers		
Brown sugar, packed	1 cup	250 mL
Butter or hard margarine	½ cup	125 mL
Milk	½ cup	125 mL
Graham cracker crumbs	1⅓ cups	325 mL
Chopped walnuts	1 cup	250 mL
Medium coconut	1 cup	250 mL
Chopped maraschino cherries, well-drained	¼ cup	60 mL
ICING		
Icing (confectioner's) sugar	1½ cups	375 mL
Butter or hard margarine, softened	3 tbsp.	50 mL
Milk	1½ tbsp.	25 mL
Vanilla	½ tsp.	2 mL
Red food coloring		

Line ungreased 9 x 9 inch (22 x 22 cm) pan with crackers, trimming to fit. Set aside.

In saucepan combine sugar, butter and milk. Bring to boil. Simmer for 2 minutes. Remove from heat.

Add graham crumbs, walnuts, coconut and cherries, stirring to mix. Pour over crackers in pan. Cool.

Icing: Beat all 5 ingredients together in small bowl adjusting liquid or icing sugar if required for proper spreading consistency and adding enough color to tint a pretty pink. Ice bars and allow to stand for several hours. Cuts into 36 squares.

Pictured on page 53.

MILLIONAIRE SQUARES

Millionaire means rich and that is exactly what these squares are.

BOTTOM LAYER

Butter or hard margarine	½ cup	125 mL
Finely crushed oatmeal cookies (Dad's is good)	2 cups	500 mL

FILLING

Semisweet chocolate baking squares, cut up (or ½ cup, 125 mL chips)	3 x 1 oz.	3 x 28 g
Butter or hard margarine	½ cup	125 mL
Large egg	1	1
Icing (confectioner's) sugar	2 cups	500 mL
Chopped walnuts (optional)	½ cup	125 mL

Reserved crumbs for topping

Bottom Layer: Melt butter in saucepan on medium-low. Stir in crushed cookies. Measure ¼ cup (60 mL) crumbs and set aside for topping. Press remaining crumbs in ungreased 8 x 8 inch (20 x 20 cm) pan. Bake in 350°F (175°) oven for 5 minutes. Cool. This baking step can be omitted if you make crust ahead and allow it to stand a few hours to harden and dry. When crust is baked first, the filling is much easier to spread without the crumbs lifting.

Filling: Melt chocolate and butter over low heat, stirring often, until smooth. Remove from heat. Add egg and beat. Add icing sugar, beating until smooth. If too soft to hold shape, add ¼ cup (60 mL) more icing sugar. This will set up a bit when chilled but not much more than when you spread it in the pan.

After filling is smoothed over crust, sprinkle with reserved crumbs. Refrigerate. Cuts into 36 small squares or 25 larger.

Pictured on page 17.

MARSHMALLOW SQUARES

The flavor and texture of these are delicious. They are among the first to disappear on a plate of dainties.

BOTTOM LAYER
All-purpose flour	1½ cups	375 mL
Brown sugar, packed	⅓ cup	75 mL
Butter, softened (see Note)	¾ cup	175 mL

SECOND LAYER
Cold water	¾ cup	175 mL
Unflavored gelatin	1 × ¼ oz.	1 × 7 g
Granulated sugar	¾ cup	175 mL
Salt	⅛ tsp.	0.5 mL
Icing (confectioner's) sugar	¾ cup	175 mL
Baking powder	¾ tsp.	4 mL
Vanilla	½ tsp.	2 mL
Almond flavoring	½ tsp.	2 mL
Red food coloring	½ tsp.	2 mL

Bottom Layer: Combine all 3 ingredients together. Mix to crumble. Press in ungreased 9 × 9 inch (22 × 22 cm) pan. Bake in 325°F (160°C) oven for 20 to 25 minutes until set. Cool.

Second Layer: Put water in saucepan. Sprinkle gelatin over top and let stand for 1 minute. Add sugar and stir. Dissolve over medium heat. Remove from heat.

Stir in icing sugar. Cool.

Beat until foamy. Add baking powder, vanilla and almond flavoring. Add food coloring to tint a pretty pink. Beat at high speed until thick enough to stand in peaks. Pour soft pink mixture over shortbread base. Cool until gloss disappears. Cuts into 36 squares.

Pictured on page 89.

Variation: Add ½ cup (125 mL) chopped candied cherries and/or ½ cup (125 mL) toasted chopped almonds.

Note: This is a shortbread base which is better made with butter. However, hard margarine, softened, could be used.

HERMIT SLICE

Just like your favorite cookie. Not too rich and not too sweet.

Butter or hard margarine, softened	¼ cup	60 mL
Granulated sugar	¼ cup	60 mL
Molasses	¼ cup	60 mL
Large egg	1	1
Raisins	½ cup	125 mL
Chopped walnuts	¼ cup	60 mL
All-purpose flour	¾ cup	175 mL
Salt	¼ tsp.	1 mL
Baking soda	⅛ tsp.	0.5 mL
Baking powder	1 tsp.	5 mL
Ground cinnamon	½ tsp.	2 mL
Ground cloves	¼ tsp.	1 mL
Ground mace	⅛ tsp.	0.5 mL
Ground nutmeg	⅛ tsp.	0.5 mL
Ground allspice	⅛ tsp.	0.5 mL
ICING		
Butter or hard margarine	3 tbsp.	50 mL
Brown sugar, packed	⅓ cup	75 mL
Milk	2 tbsp.	30 mL
Icing (confectioner's) sugar	1 cup	250 mL

In large bowl beat together butter, sugar, molasses and egg. Add raisins and walnuts. Stir to mix.

Measure in flour, salt, baking soda, baking powder and spices. Stir well. Spread in greased 8 x 8 inch (20 x 20 cm) pan. Bake in 350°F (175°C) oven for 20 minutes until set. Cool.

Icing: Combine butter, brown sugar and milk in saucepan. Bring to a boil and simmer 2 minutes. Allow to cool until you can hold your hand on bottom of pan.

Add icing sugar and stir well. If too firm to spread add a few drops of milk. If too runny add a bit more icing sugar. Spread over squares. Cuts into 25 squares.

Pictured on page 71.

LEMON SLICE

Very showy with a light-textured chiffon topping.

BOTTOM LAYER		
Butter or hard margarine	½ cup	125 mL
Graham cracker crumbs	2 cups	500 mL
Granulated sugar	¼ cup	60 mL
SECOND LAYER		
Granulated sugar	¾ cup	175 mL
All-purpose flour	⅓ cup	75 mL
Water	1 tbsp.	15 mL
Egg yolks (large)	3	3
Fresh lemon, grated rind and juice	1	1
Egg whites (large), room temperature	3	3
Handful of graham cracker crumbs	1	1

Bottom Layer: Melt butter in medium saucepan. Stir in graham crumbs and sugar. Press in ungreased 9 x 9 inch (22 x 22 cm) pan. Bake in 350°F (175°C) oven for 10 minutes.

Second Layer: In double boiler combine sugar, flour, water, egg yolks, grated rind and lemon juice. Cook and stir over boiling water until thickened. If using heavy pan instead, be sure to stir continually. Remove from heat.

Beat egg whites in small mixing bowl until stiff. Fold into hot thickened mixture. Spread over bottom layer.

Sprinkle with graham crumbs. Bake in 350°F (175°C) oven for 3 to 5 minutes or until set. Cuts into 36 squares.

Pictured on cover.

GINGER SHORTBREAD

One of the first stories I can remember from a young grade was of Pung Gee in a ginger factory and how he hated ginger. Oh well!

Butter (do not use margarine), softened	1 cup	250 mL
Icing (confectioner's) sugar	½ cup	125 mL
All-purpose flour	2 cups	500 mL
Chopped candied ginger	¼-½ cup	60-125 mL
Ground ginger (if desired for stronger ginger flavor)	1 tsp.	5 mL
Ground ginger, sprinkle		

Measure first 3 ingredients in bowl. Cut butter into icing sugar and flour, ending up mixing with your hands as for pie crust.

When mixture will hold together, work in chopped ginger and ground ginger, if using. Press in ungreased 9 x 9 inch (22 x 22 cm) pan about ½ inch (1 cm) thick. Prick with fork through to the bottom of batter. Bake in 300°F (150°C) oven for 50 to 60 minutes until a delicate golden color.

Sprinkle with ground ginger. Cut while warm into 36 squares.

Pictured on page 71.

BANANA OAT SQUARES

A rich looking, healthy bar.

Butter or hard margarine, softened	6 tbsp.	100 mL
Brown sugar, packed	½ cup	125 mL
Large egg	1	1
Salt	¼ tsp.	1 mL
Mashed bananas (about 3)	¾ cup	175 mL
Quick-cooking rolled oats	2 cups	450 mL
Chopped walnuts	⅓ cup	75 mL

Cream butter and sugar. Add egg and beat well. Add salt and mashed banana. Beat. Add rolled oats and walnuts. Stir. Spread in greased 8 x 8 inch (20 x 20 cm) pan. Bake in 350°F (175°C) oven for 50 to 60 minutes, until firm. Cool. Cuts into 25 squares.

Pictured on page 71.

MATRIMONIAL SQUARES

Favorite date squares that are not nearly as messy to eat as some others. These crumbs hold together well.

CRUMB LAYERS
All-purpose flour	1¼ cups	300 mL
Rolled oats	1½ cups	375 mL
Brown sugar, packed	1 cup	250 mL
Baking soda	1 tsp.	5 mL
Salt	½ tsp.	2 mL
Butter or hard margarine, softened	1 cup	250 mL

FILLING
Chopped dates	1½ cups	375 mL
Granulated sugar	½ cup	125 mL
Water	⅔ cup	150 mL

Crumb Layers: Measure flour, rolled oats, sugar, baking soda, salt and butter into large bowl. Cut in butter until crumbly. Press a generous ½ in greased 9 x 9 inch (22 x 22 cm) pan.

Filling: In saucepan combine dates, sugar and water. Bring to a boil and allow to simmer until mushy. If mixture becomes too dry before dates have softened, add more water. If you find you have too much water, simmer until some has boiled away. Spread over bottom layer of crumbs. Sprinkle remaining crumbs over top. Press down with your hand. Bake in 350°F (175°C) oven for 30 minutes until a rich golden brown color. Cuts into 36 squares.

Pictured on page 143.

BLACK BOTTOM SLICE

The cocoa in the bottom layer makes a nice change from the usual.

BOTTOM LAYER		
Butter or hard margarine, softened	½ cup	125 mL
Cocoa	¼ cup	60 mL
Granulated sugar	¼ cup	60 mL
All-purpose flour	1 cup	250 mL
FILLING		
Large eggs	2	2
Brown sugar, packed	1¼ cups	300 mL
All-purpose flour	1 tsp.	5 mL
Baking powder	1 tsp.	5 mL
Vanilla	1 tsp.	5 mL
Medium coconut	1 cup	250 mL
Chopped walnuts	¾ cup	175 mL
ICING		
Icing (confectioner's) sugar	1¼ cups	300 mL
Cocoa	¼ cup	60 mL
Butter or hard margarine, softened	3 tbsp.	50 mL
Hot prepared coffee	1½ tbsp.	25 mL

Bottom Layer: Crumble all ingredients together and press in ungreased 9 x 9 inch (22 x 22 cm) pan. Bake in 350°F (175°C) oven for 15 minutes.

Filling: Beat eggs until frothy. Add sugar, flour, baking powder, vanilla, coconut and walnuts. Stir to combine. Spread over bottom layer. Bake in 350°F (175°C) oven for 30 minutes. Cool.

Icing: Measure all 4 ingredients into small bowl. Beat well. Add more liquid or icing sugar as needed for easy spreading. Spread over cooled bars. Cuts into 36 squares.

Pictured on page 89.

NUTTY BARS

These squares are not as sweet as most and are the nuttiest you could wish for.

Large egg	1	1
Brown sugar, packed	1 cup	250 mL
Vanilla	1 tsp.	5 mL
All-purpose flour	½ cup	125 mL
Salt	¼ tsp.	1 mL
Baking soda	¼ tsp.	1 mL
Chopped walnuts	1 cup	250 mL

Beat egg slightly in bowl. Add sugar and vanilla. Stir. Mix in flour, salt, baking soda and walnuts. Spread in greased 8 x 8 inch (20 x 20 cm) pan. Bake in 350°F (175°C) oven for 20 minutes. Cuts into 25 squares.

Pictured on page 125.

1. Oh Henry Bars page 44
2. Chocolate Crisps page 10
3. Puffed Wheat Squares page 26
4. Chocolate Confetti page 28
5. Midnight Mints page 13
6. Rice Krispies page 9
7. Chocolate Oh Henry Squares page 42
8. S'Mores page 10
9. Jellied Marshmallows page 26

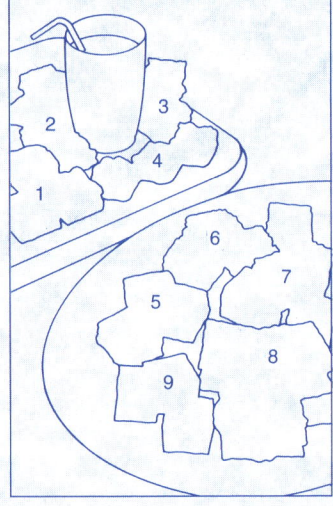

Wooden Board Courtesy Of:
The Bay Housewares Dept.

Platter Courtesy Of:
Eaton's Housewares Dept.

Tiles Courtesy Of:
Edmonton Tile Centre

FRUIT MARMALADE SQUARES

This is a glistening, fruity bar. Watch that you don't overcook it or it will be too chewy.

BOTTOM LAYER
Butter or hard margarine, softened	½ cup	125 mL
Granulated sugar	¼ cup	60 mL
Egg yolk (large)	1	1
All-purpose flour	1¼ cups	300 mL

SECOND LAYER
Large egg	1	1
Marmalade	¼ cup	60 mL
Milk	2 tbsp.	30 mL
Granulated sugar	¼ cup	60 mL
Chopped dates	¾ cup	175 mL
Raisins	¾ cup	175 mL
Chopped walnuts	½ cup	125 mL

Red and green candied cherries, halved

Bottom Layer: Crumble all 4 ingredients together well. Press in ungreased 9 x 9 inch (22 x 22 cm) pan. Bake in 350° (175°C) oven for 15 minutes.

Second Layer: In large bowl beat egg until frothy. Beat in marmalade and milk. Stir in sugar, dates, raisins and walnuts. Spread over bottom layer. Bake in 350°F (175°C) oven for 25 minutes until set.

Decorate with cherries when squares are just out of the oven. Cool. Store in airtight container. Cuts into 36 squares.

Pictured on page 125.

Going on a fishing trip? Better eat everything now you can get your hands on. How do you know that you will catch any fish?

SCOTCH SHORTBREAD

A favorite recipe for shortbread, that always turns out.

Butter (do not use margarine)	1 cup	250 mL
Icing (confectioner's) sugar (see Note)	½ cup	125 mL
All-purpose flour	2 cups	500 mL

Combine all ingredients in large bowl. Work with pastry cutter and cut in butter until mixture is mealy. With your hands, mix until you get a smooth ball. Press flat in ungreased 9 x 9 inch (22 x 22 cm) pan. Prick all over with fork right through to the bottom. Bake in 300°F (150°C) oven for 50 to 60 minutes until set and very pale gold. Cut while warm into 36 squares.

Note: Use same amount of granulated sugar in place of icing sugar if preferred.

Pictured on page 143.

CRANBERRY OAT SQUARES

After you have served turkey or chicken and you find that you have too much cranberry on hand, try this. Good served hot with ice cream.

Rolled oats	1½ cups	375 mL
All-purpose flour	1½ cups	375 mL
Brown sugar, packed	1 cup	250 mL
Butter or hard margarine, softened	1 cup	250 mL
Baking soda	¼ tsp.	1 mL
Whole cranberry sauce	14 oz.	398 mL

Measure rolled oats, flour, sugar, butter and baking soda into bowl. Mix together until crumbly. Pack a generous ½ of mixture in greased 9 x 9 inch (22 x 22 cm) pan.

Spread cranberry sauce over top. Sprinkle with remaining crumb mixture. Press down with your hand. Bake in 350°F (175°C) oven for 35 to 40 minutes until a rich golden brown. Cuts into 36 squares.

Pictured on page 125.

CHOCOLATE NUT SHORTCAKE

New Zealand deserves the credit for this version of a combination of several flavors.

BOTTOM LAYER		
Butter or hard margarine, softened	½ cup	125 mL
Brown sugar, packed	½ cup	125 mL
All-purpose flour	1½ cups	375 mL
Baking powder	1 tsp.	5 mL
Egg yolks (large)	2	2
FILLING		
Apricot jam	1 cup	250 mL
TOP LAYER		
Semisweet chocolate chips	½ cup	125 mL
Salted peanuts	¾ cup	175 mL
Granulated sugar	¾ cup	175 mL
Egg whites (large)	2	2

Bottom Layer: Measure all 5 ingredients into bowl. Cut in butter until mixture is mealy and crumbly in texture. Press in ungreased 9 x 9 inch (22 x 22 cm) pan.

Filling: Spread jam over bottom layer. Start with putting a dab here and there so it will be easier to spread without too many crumbs moving around.

Top Layer: In medium saucepan combine chocolate chips, peanuts, sugar and egg whites. Stir over medium heat as you bring it to a boil and chips melt. Pour over jam layer. Bake in 350°F (175°C) oven for 30 to 35 minutes until well set. Cut while hot for best results. Cuts into 36 squares.

Pictured on page 143.

NUTTY SPICE SLICE

A good keeper with a mild spicy taste. Freeze before icing or ice and eat fresh.

Raisins	½ cup	125 mL
Walnuts	½ cup	125 mL
Baking soda	½ tsp.	2 mL
Boiling water	½ cup	125 mL
Butter or hard margarine, softened	½ cup	125 mL
Brown sugar, packed	1 cup	250 mL
Large egg	1	1
Vanilla	½ tsp.	2 mL
All-purpose flour	1½ cups	375 mL
Ground cinnamon	½ tsp.	2 mL
Ground nutmeg	½ tsp.	2 mL
Baking powder	¼ tsp.	1 mL
ICING		
Icing (confectioner's) sugar	1½ cups	375 mL
Butter or hard margarine, softened	3 tbsp.	50 mL
Strong prepared coffee	1½ tbsp.	25 mL

Put raisins and walnuts through food chopper. Add baking soda. Pour on boiling water and stir. Set aside.

Beat butter, sugar, egg and vanilla together well in bowl. Add raisin mixture and stir well.

Measure in flour, cinnamon, nutmeg and baking powder. Stir to combine. Pour into greased 9 x 9 inch (22 x 22 cm) pan. Bake in 350°F (175°C) oven for 40 to 45 minutes or until an inserted wooden pick comes out clean and dry. Cool.

Icing: Beat icing sugar, butter and coffee together in small bowl adding more icing sugar or liquid if needed for spreading. Spread over squares and allow to set. Cuts into 36 squares.

Pictured on page 125.

PINEAPPLE BARS

Serve this at your Hawaiian party.

BOTTOM LAYER		
Butter or hard margarine, softened	½ cup	125 mL
Granulated sugar	¼ cup	60 mL
All-purpose flour	1¼ cups	300 mL
SECOND LAYER		
Large eggs	2	2
Brown sugar, packed	1 cup	250 mL
Crushed pineapple, drained, reserve juice for icing	1 cup	250 mL
Almond flavoring	½ tsp.	2 mL
Baking powder	½ tsp.	2 mL
Salt	¼ tsp.	1 mL
All-purpose flour	2 tbsp.	30 mL
Chopped walnuts	½ cup	125 mL
ICING		
Icing (confectioner's) sugar	1½ cups	375 mL
Butter or hard margarine, softened	3 tbsp.	50 mL
Reserved pineapple juice, from above	1½ tbsp.	25 mL

Bottom Layer: Combine butter, sugar and flour in bowl. Crumble together well. Pack in ungreased 9 x 9 inch (22 x 22 cm) pan. Bake in 350°F (175°C) oven for 15 minutes.

Second Layer: Beat eggs slightly. Add remaining ingredients. Stir to mix. Spread over shortbread base. Bake in 350°F (175°C) oven for 30 minutes or until set and a rich brown color. Cool.

Icing: Beat icing sugar, butter and juice together in bowl, adding more juice a few drops at a time to reach proper spreading consistency. Spread over bars. Cuts into 36 squares.

Pictured on page 71.

LEMON CRUNCH

Using soda crackers in this square gives it a bit of a different touch.

BOTTOM LAYER
Soda crackers, finely rolled	1⅓ cups	325 mL
Butter or hard margarine, softened	¾ cup	175 mL
Granulated sugar	½ cup	125 mL
All purpose-flour	¾ cup	175 mL
Medium coconut	½ cup	125 mL
Baking powder	1 tsp.	5 mL

FILLING
Large eggs, beaten	3	3
Lemon, grated rind and juice	1	1
Granulated sugar	1 cup	250 mL
Butter or hard margarine	¼ cup	60 mL

Bottom Layer: Crumble all ingredients together. Remove 1 cup (250 mL) of crumbs for topping. Press remaining crumbs into greased 9 x 9 inch (22 x 22 cm) pan. Bake in 350°F (175°C) oven for 15 minutes. Remove from oven.

Filling: Beat eggs in top of double boiler or heavy pot. Add remaining ingredients. Stir and cook until thickened. Spread over crumbs in pan. Sprinkle reserved crumbs over top. Return to oven until browned slightly. Cool. Cuts into 36 squares.

Pictured on page 107.

In case of a natural disaster it is the duty of every citizen to have an extra supply of calories stored up.

BUTTERSCOTCH BROWNIES

A chewy brownie with a caramel flavor.

Butter or hard margarine	¼ cup	60 mL
Brown sugar, packed	1 cup	250 mL
Large egg	1	1
Vanilla	½ tsp.	2 mL
All-purpose flour	¾ cup	175 mL
Baking powder	1 tsp.	5 mL
Salt	¼ tsp.	1 mL
Chopped walnuts	½ cup	125 mL
ICING		
Butter or hard margarine	2 tbsp.	30 mL
Brown sugar, packed	¼ cup	60 mL
Milk	2 tbsp.	30 mL
Icing (confectioner's) sugar	1 cup	250 mL

Melt butter in saucepan and add it to sugar in bowl. Stir. Add egg and vanilla and stir.

Measure in flour, baking powder, salt and walnuts. Mix well. Spread in greased 8 x 8 inch (20 x 20 cm) pan. Bake in 350°F (175°C) oven for 30 minutes until sides show signs of pulling away from the pan. A wooden pick inserted in center should come out moist but with no batter clinging to it. Cool.

Icing: Combine first 3 ingredients in saucepan. Bring to a boil and simmer 2 minutes. Remove from heat. Cool.

Add icing sugar and stir well. Add more icing sugar or milk as needed to make a smooth spreadable icing. Spread over brownies. Cuts into 25 squares.

Pictured on page 125.

FRUITY FRUIT SLICE

This calls for a bit more time than usual to get ready for the oven with putting the cherries on top, but then you need not ice it.

Large eggs, beaten	2	2
Lemon flavoring	¼ tsp.	1 mL
Chopped dates	1 cup	250 mL
Granulated sugar	½ cup	125 mL
Cut mixed fruit peel	½ cup	125 mL
Chopped walnuts	1 cup	250 mL
All-purpose flour	6 tbsp.	100 mL
Baking powder	1 tsp.	5 mL
Salt	½ tsp.	2 mL
Red and green candied cherries	13	13

Beat eggs in bowl until frothy. Add next 8 ingredients in order given. Mix and put into greased 8 x 8 inch (20 x 20 cm) pan.

Cut cherries in half. Put cut side of cherries down on top allowing 1 per square. If you cut 5 x 5 you need 25 halves or 13 cherries. Alternate colors. Bake in 350°F (175°C) oven for 25 to 30 minutes. Cuts into 25 squares.

Pictured on page 89.

Be sure to consume all the buns, butter and other extras that come with the meal in a restaurant, such as the soup and dessert. Fight inflation. Don't waste a thing.

CARIBBEAN BARS

With the pineapple and touch of rum, this is well-named.

BOTTOM LAYER		
Butter or hard margarine, softened	½ cup	125 mL
Granulated sugar	¼ cup	60 mL
All-purpose flour	1¼ cups	300 mL

SECOND LAYER		
Large eggs	2	2
Brown sugar, packed	1 cup	250 mL
Crushed pineapple, drained, reserve juice for icing	½ cup	125 mL
Medium coconut	1 cup	250 mL
Chopped candied cherries	⅓ cup	75 mL
Rum flavoring	1 tsp.	5 mL
All-purpose flour	2 tbsp.	30 mL
Baking powder	½ tsp.	2 mL

ICING		
Icing (confectioner's) sugar	1½ cups	375 mL
Butter or hard margarine, softened	3 tbsp.	50 mL
Rum flavoring	½ tsp.	2 mL
Reserved pineapple juice	1½ tbsp.	25 mL

Bottom Layer: Crumble butter, sugar and flour together well. Pack in ungreased 9 x 9 inch (22 x 22 cm) pan. Bake in 350°F (175°C) oven for 15 minutes.

Second Layer: Beat eggs slightly. Stir in remaining ingredients. Spread over bottom layer. Bake in 350°F (175°C) oven for 25 to 30 minutes until set and a medium brown color. Cool.

Icing: Combine all 4 ingredients in bowl. Beat, adding more juice if icing is too stiff. Spread over bars. Allow to set before cutting. Cuts into 36 squares.

Pictured on page 143.

CHOCOLATE CHERRY SLICE

A smooth chocolate bottom layer makes the difference. Try this one and see how long you can keep it around.

BOTTOM LAYER
Sweet chocolate baking squares (or use 1⅓ cups, 325 mL sweet chocolate chips)	8 × 1 oz.	8 × 28 g

SECOND LAYER
Large eggs	2	2
Granulated sugar	½ cup	125 mL
Medium coconut	1½ cups	375 mL
Chopped candied cherries	¼ cup	60 mL

Icing (confectioner's) sugar

Bottom Layer: Put chocolate in top of double boiler over hot (not boiling) water to melt, stirring once in awhile to hasten it. When melted pour into greased 8 × 8 inch (20 × 20 cm) pan. Chill.

Second Layer: Beat eggs and sugar together until frothy and thick. Fold in coconut and cherries. Spread over cooled chocolate layer. Bake in 350°F (175°C) oven for 25 to 30 minutes until a golden color and firm to the touch. Cool. Store in refrigerator.

Before serving, sift icing sugar over top. Cuts into 25 squares.

Pictured on cover.

Those two are always cooking up something but rarely on the stove.

CARAMEL SLICE

This is an exceptionally good square. With its caramel taste and lots of nuts, there isn't anyone who doesn't like it.

Butter or hard margarine	¼ cup	60 mL
Brown sugar, packed	1 cup	250 mL
Large eggs, beaten	2	2
Chopped walnuts	½ cup	125 mL
All-purpose flour	¾ cup	175 mL
Baking powder	1 tsp.	5 mL
Salt	¼ tsp.	1 mL
Medium coconut	1 cup	250 mL
ICING		
Butter or hard margarine	¼ cup	60 mL
Brown sugar, packed	½ cup	125 mL
Milk	2 tbsp.	30 mL
Icing (confectioner's) sugar	1 cup	250 mL

Melt butter in large saucepan. Remove from heat. Add sugar. Stir in beaten eggs.

Measure in walnuts, flour, baking powder, salt and coconut. Stir well. Scrape into greased 9 x 9 inch (22 x 22 cm) pan. Bake in 350°F (175°C) oven for 20 to 25 minutes or until set and a light brown color. Cool.

Icing: Combine butter, sugar and milk in saucepan. Bring to a boil and simmer 2 minutes. Cool. To speed up this procedure, run some cold water in sink. Set pan in water. Stir until cool.

Stir in icing sugar. If too stiff, add a bit more milk until soft enough to spread. If too thin add more icing sugar. Smooth over bars. Let set. Cuts into 36 squares.

Pictured on cover.

BANANA BARS

There are not many squares with bananas in them. Of those familiar to us, this is one of the taste pleasers.

Butter or hard margarine, softened	¼ cup	60 mL
Brown sugar, packed	½ cup	125 mL
Large egg	1	1
Vanilla	½ tsp.	2 mL
Mashed bananas (2 small)	½ cup	125 mL
Apricot jam	⅓ cup	75 mL
Lemon juice, fresh or bottled	1 tsp.	5 mL
All-purpose flour	1 cup	250 mL
Baking powder	½ tsp.	2 mL
Salt	¼ tsp.	1 mL
Chopped walnuts	¼ cup	60 mL
Apricot jam, sieved	¼ cup	60 mL
Crushed or ground walnuts	¼ cup	60 mL

Cream butter with sugar. Add egg and vanilla. Beat until fluffy. Stir in banana, first amount of jam and lemon juice. Stir in flour, baking powder, salt and first amount of walnuts. Spread in greased 9 x 9 inch (22 x 22 cm) pan. Bake in 350°F (175°C) oven for 25 to 30 minutes. Remove from oven.

Spread immediately with sieved jam. Sprinkle with crushed walnuts. Cool. Cuts into 36 squares.

Pictured on page 89.

Don't ever eat like a rabbit with all that so-called rabbit food. Bigger animals eat them for dinner. Defend yourself. Eat lots.

FESTIVE FRUIT CAKE

This has to be the next best thing to a Christmas cake yet it bakes in a fraction of the time.

All-purpose flour	¼ cup	60 mL
Cut mixed candied fruit	⅔ cup	150 mL
Butter or hard margarine, softened	½ cup	125 mL
Granulated sugar	½ cup	125 mL
Frozen concentrated orange juice	2 tbsp.	30 mL
Grated orange rind	1 tsp.	5 mL
Large egg	1	1
Almond flavoring	¼ tsp.	1 mL
All-purpose flour	1½ cups	375 mL
Baking soda	½ tsp.	2 mL
Salt	¼ tsp.	1 mL
Chopped walnuts	½ cup	125 mL
ICING		
Icing (confectioner's) sugar	1½ cups	375 mL
Butter or hard margarine, softened	3 tbsp.	50 mL
Prepared orange juice	1½ tbsp.	25 mL

Stir first amount of flour into candied fruit to coat each piece.

In another bowl, cream butter and sugar. Add orange juice and rind. Beat until well blended. Beat in egg until very well combined. Stir in almond flavoring. Measure in second amount of flour, baking soda and salt, stirring to mix. Fold in fruit and walnuts. Scrape into greased 9 x 9 inch (22 x 22 cm) pan. Bake in 350°F (175°C) oven for 20 minutes until it shows signs of pulling away from sides of pan. Cool.

Icing: Beat all 3 ingredients together adding a bit more juice if necessary. Spread over cooled bars Cuts into 36 squares.

Pictured on page 125.

MARBLE SQUARES

This takes a bit more time to make but anything so rich is bound to be worthwhile!

Large eggs	2	2
Granulated sugar	¼ cup	60 mL
Brown sugar, packed	1 cup	250 mL
All-purpose flour	¾ cup	175 mL
Baking powder	½ tsp.	2 mL
Vanilla	1 tsp.	5 mL
Salt	⅛ tsp.	0.5 mL
Medium coconut	½ cup	125 mL
Unsweetened chocolate baking square, cut up	1 × 1 oz.	1 × 28 g
Butter or hard margarine	1 tbsp.	15 mL
Chopped walnuts	¼ cup	60 mL
Large marshmallows, cut in half (use scissors)	18	18
ICING		
Icing (confectioner's) sugar	1⅓ cups	325 mL
Butter or hard margarine, softened	2 tbsp.	30 mL
Cocoa	⅓ cup	75 mL
Water	1½ tbsp.	25 mL

Beat eggs slightly. Add both sugars, flour, baking powder, vanilla and salt. Stir well. Divide batter into 2 portions.

To 1 part add coconut and mix well. Spread in greased 9 × 9 inch (22 × 22 cm) pan.

Melt chocolate and butter in saucepan on low heat, stirring often. Add walnuts. Add to second portion of batter. Mix and spread over first layer in pan. Bake in 350°F (175°C) oven for 30 minutes or until cooked.

Remove from oven and cover with marshmallow halves, putting 6 one way and 6 along the other making 36 halves in all. Return to oven for 2 minutes. Remove. Use point of knife to spread marshmallows evenly.

Icing: Beat all 4 ingredients in bowl. Add more water if needed so the icing will spread. Smooth over warm squares. Cool. Cuts into 36 squares.

Pictured on page 125.

PINEAPPLE BROWNIES

A good moist variation for brownies.

Butter or hard margarine	½ cup	125 mL
Unsweetened chocolate baking squares	2 × 1 oz.	2 × 28 g
Granulated sugar	1 cup	250 mL
Large eggs	2	2
Crushed pineapple, drained, reserve juice for icing	½ cup	125 mL
All-purpose flour	1 cup	250 mL
Vanilla	½ tsp.	2 mL
Baking powder	½ tsp.	2 mL
Baking soda	¼ tsp.	1 mL
Salt	½ tsp.	2 mL
Chopped walnuts	½ cup	125 mL
ICING		
Icing (confectioner's) sugar	1½ cups	375 mL
Butter or hard margarine, softened	3 tbsp.	50 mL
Reserved pineapple juice	1½ tbsp.	25 mL

Combine butter and chocolate in saucepan and melt over low heat, stirring often.

In bowl beat sugar and eggs together. Add chocolate mixture.

Stir in pineapple. Measure in flour, vanilla, baking powder, baking soda, salt and walnuts. Stir well. Scrape into greased 9 × 9 inch (22 × 22 cm) pan. Bake in 350°F (175°C) oven for 30 minutes until edges show signs of pulling away from pan. Cool.

Icing: Beat all 3 ingredients together in small bowl adding more icing sugar or juice as needed for easy spreading. Smooth over brownies. Cut when set. Cuts into 36 squares.

Pictured on page 35.

APPLE SQUARES

This is sort of like a cake, with little pits made when the apple cooks and shrinks.

Butter or hard margarine, softened	6 tbsp.	100 mL
Large eggs	2	2
Granulated sugar	1 cup	250 mL
Baking soda	1 tsp.	5 mL
Vanilla	1 tsp.	5 mL
Ground cinnamon	¼ tsp.	1 mL
All-purpose flour	1 cup	250 mL
Peeled and chopped cooking apples (such as McIntosh)	2 cups	500 mL
Chopped walnuts	½ cup	125 mL

Icing (confectioner's) sugar

Combine butter, eggs, sugar, baking soda, vanilla, cinnamon and flour in large bowl. Beat until well mixed.

Add apple and walnuts. Stir to mix. Scrape into greased 9 x 9 inch (22 x 22 cm) pan. Bake in 350°F (175°C) oven for 40 to 50 minutes. Cool 15 minutes.

Sift icing sugar over top. Cuts into 36 squares.

Pictured on page 143.

1. Hermit Slice page 47
2. Chocolate Walnut Slice page 84
3. Pineapple Bars page 59
4. Raspberry Bars page 94
5. Tweed Squares page 100
6. Peanut Krispie Squares page 41
7. Chocolate Date Nut Squares page 88
8. Five-Cup Slice page 78
9. Coconut Graham Cake page 85
10. Chip Crumbles page 82
11. Cherry Squares page 92
12. Ginger Shortbread page 49
13. Mincemeat Squares page 75
14. Banana Oat Squares page 49
15. Peanut Butter Bars page 82
16. Gumdrop Bars page 78

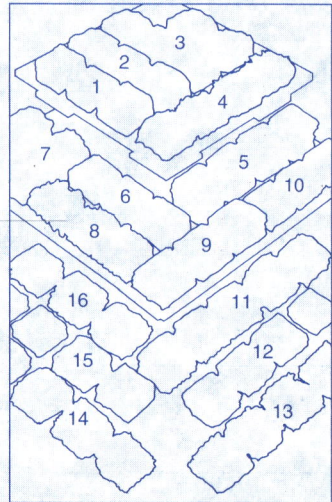

Trays Courtesy Of:
Ali Katu

MARZIPAN BARS

A festive almond-flavored, pretty square. It takes a little longer than usual to put in the pan but the end result is well worth it.

BOTTOM LAYER
Pie crust, your own or a mix, enough for 1 crust

FILLING
Raspberry jam	¼ cup	60 mL

TOP LAYER
Butter or hard margarine, softened	½ cup	125 mL
Granulated sugar	⅔ cup	150 mL
Large eggs	2	2
Rice flour	½ cup	125 mL
Salt	¼ tsp.	1 mL
Red food coloring		
Green food coloring		

ICING
Icing (confectioner's) sugar	1½ cups	375 mL
Butter or hard margarine, softened	3 tbsp.	50 mL
Almond flavoring	1 tsp.	5 mL
Milk	1½ tbsp.	25 mL

Bottom Layer: Roll out pie crust and press in bottom of ungreased 9 x 9 inch (22 x 22 cm) pan.

Filling: Spread jam thinly over bottom crust.

Top Layer: Beat butter and sugar together in medium bowl. Add eggs 1 at a time, beating well after each addition. When fluffy, stir in rice flour and salt. Divide batter into 2 equal portions. Tint 1 portion pink and the other green. Place on top of jam layer, alternating teaspoonfuls of each color. This will look like a checkerboard when finished. Bake on lower rack in 375°F (190°C) oven for about 30 minutes. Do not try to brown. It will spread flat as it cooks. Cool.

Icing: Beat all 4 ingredients together, adding more liquid or icing sugar as needed for proper spreading consistency. Spread over cooled bars. Cuts into 36 squares.

Pictured on page 125.

DOUBLE BROWNIES

This way you get both — chocolate and butterscotch in every piece.

CHOCOLATE LAYER		
Large eggs	2	2
Granulated sugar	1 cup	250 mL
All-purpose flour	¾ cup	175 mL
Chopped walnuts	½ cup	125 mL
Salt	⅛ tsp.	0.5 mL
Cocoa	¼ cup	60 mL
Butter or hard margarine	½ cup	125 mL
BUTTERSCOTCH LAYER		
Butter or hard margarine, softened	½ cup	125 mL
Brown sugar, packed	1½ cups	375 mL
Large eggs	2	2
Vanilla	2 tsp.	10 mL
All-purpose flour	1½ cups	375 mL
Salt	¼ tsp.	1 mL
Chopped walnuts	½ cup	125 mL
ICING		
Butter or hard margarine	¼ cup	60 mL
Brown sugar, packed	½ cup	125 mL
Milk	3 tbsp.	50 mL
Icing (confectioner's) sugar	1½ cups	375 mL
Semisweet chocolate chips	⅔ cup	150 mL
Butter or hard margarine	1 tbsp.	15 mL

Chocolate Layer: Beat eggs until foamy. Add sugar, flour, walnuts and salt.

Melt cocoa and butter together in saucepan over low heat. Add to egg mixture and blend well. Spread in greased 9 x 13 inch (22 x 33 cm) pan. Set aside.

Butterscotch Layer: Cream butter with brown sugar in another bowl. Add eggs and vanilla. Beat until well mixed. Add remaining ingredients. Stir. Spoon over chocolate layer in small blobs. Spread as best you can. Bake in 350°F (175°C) oven for about 35 minutes until brownies begin to pull away from sides of pan. A wooden pick inserted in center should come out moist with no batter clinging to it. Cool.

(continued on next page)

Icing: Bring butter, brown sugar and milk to boil in saucepan. Simmer for 2 minutes. Cool.

Stir in icing sugar, adding more sugar or milk if necessary to make consistency for easy spreading. Spread over cooled squares.

Melt chocolate chips and butter together in top of double boiler over hot (not boiling) water to melt, stirring often. Drizzle over icing. Cuts into 54 squares.

Pictured on page 143.

MINCEMEAT SQUARES

This is especially good if you have any homemade mincemeat. It has a slightly spicy taste and is very moist.

BOTTOM LAYER		
All-purpose flour	1½ cups	375 mL
Rolled oats	½ cup	125 mL
Butter or hard margarine, softened	¾ cup	175 mL
Brown sugar, packed	½ cup	125 mL
FILLING		
Mincemeat	1 cup	250 mL

TOP LAYER
Reserved crumb mixture
Icing (confectioner's) sugar, optional

Bottom Layer: Measure flour, rolled oats, butter and brown sugar into bowl. Mix until crumbly. Pack ⅔ of crumbs in bottom of ungreased 9 x 9 inch (22 x 22 cm) pan.

Filling: Put mincemeat in blender to smooth. Spread over bottom layer in pan.

Top Layer: Sprinkle the last ⅓ of the crumbs over the mincemeat layer. Pack down gently with your hand. Bake in 350°F (175°C) oven for 25 to 30 minutes until set and a nice golden color. Cool. Dust with icing sugar if desired. Cuts into 36 squares.

Pictured on page 71.

CHEESE APPLE SQUARES

You know how cheese and apple go together!

Grated medium Cheddar cheese	1 cup	250 mL
Butter or hard margarine, softened	½ cup	125 mL
All-purpose flour	1½ cups	375 mL
Baking powder	1 tsp.	5 mL
Granulated sugar	2 tbsp.	30 mL
Apple or crabapple jelly or canned apple pie filling	1 cup	250 mL
GLAZE		
Apple jelly	¼ cup	60 mL

Crumble cheese and butter together well. Add flour, baking powder and sugar. A food processor works well. Continue to crumble well. Spread generous ½ of mixture in greased 8 x 8 inch (20 x 20 cm) pan.

Spread with apple jelly. Cover with remaining mixture. Press lightly with your hand. Bake in 350°F (175°F) oven for 30 minutes.

Glaze: Melt apple jelly and smooth over top of bars. Much easier to do while hot by dabbing it on directly from container and spreading as it melts. Cool. Wrap airtight.

Pictured on page 143.

Eat more and live longer. Look at the whale and the elephant. Eat like a fly and you're dead in two weeks!

CHERRY TRIANGLES

You will find this a very different square. There is only the slightest hint of sweetness. The yeast lends its own flavor and the center ribbon of red makes it quite an eye-catcher.

Milk	⅔ cup	150 mL
Granulated sugar	1 tsp.	5 mL
Envelope dry yeast granules (1 tbsp., 15 mL)	1 x ¼ oz.	1 x 8 g
Butter or hard margarine, softened	1 cup	250 mL
All-purpose flour	2½ cups	625 mL
Egg yolks (large), slightly beaten	4	4
Canned cherry pie filling	19 oz.	540 mL
Minute tapioca	2 tbsp.	30 mL
ICING		
Icing (confectioner's) sugar	1½ cups	375 mL
Butter or hard margarine, softened	3 tbsp.	50 mL
Water	1½ tbsp.	25 mL
Vanilla	½ tsp.	2 mL
Finely chopped walnuts	2 tbsp.	30 mL
Chopped cherries (optional)	2 tbsp.	30 mL

Pour milk into small saucepan. Bring just to below boiling in order to scald. Remove from heat. Cool to lukewarm. Discard the skin that will have formed as milk has cooled.

Stir in sugar. Sprinkle yeast over top being very careful not to let any granules stick to sides of pan or you will have solid little bits of yeast in crust. Let stand for 10 minutes. Stir. Pour yeast mixture into bowl.

Add butter and stir. Add flour and egg yolks. Mix together to make smooth dough. Press out ½ of dough in bottom of greased 9 x 13 inch (22 x 33 cm) pan. Dip fingers in flour as you press.

Combine cherry pie filling with tapioca. Spread over bottom crust. Press out ½ of top crust on floured surface. Put on top of pie filling. Repeat for second ½ of top crust. Dampen center edge with water. Pinch to seal together. Bake in 350°F (175°C) oven for 45 to 50 minutes. Cool.

Icing: Beat icing sugar, butter, water and vanilla together well, adding a bit more water or icing sugar if needed for easy spreading. Smooth over cooled squares.

Sprinkle with chopped walnuts, and cherries, if desired. Cuts into 54 squares.

Pictured on cover.

FIVE-CUP SLICE

Another of those quick easy bars everyone likes.

Raisins	1¼ cups	300 mL
Semisweet chocolate chips	1¼ cups	300 mL
Peanuts	1¼ cups	300 mL
Medium coconut	1¼ cups	300 mL
Sweetened condensed milk	11 oz.	300 mL

Coarsely chop raisins, if you like. It is not necessary but flavor is improved. Combine all ingredients in bowl. Stir well to mix. Spread in greased 9 x 9 inch (22 x 22 cm) pan. Bake in 350°F (175°C) oven for 25 to 30 minutes. Cuts into 36 squares.

Pictured on page 71.

GUMDROP BARS

Here is a substitution for cut fruit — gumdrop candies. Has a caramel flavor.

Butter or hard margarine, softened	⅓ cup	75 mL
Brown sugar, packed	⅓ cup	75 mL
Granulated sugar	½ cup	125 mL
Large eggs, beaten	2	2
All-purpose flour	1 cup	225 mL
Salt	¼ tsp.	1 mL
Rolled oats	1 cup	225 mL
Baking powder	½ tsp.	2 mL
Baking soda	½ tsp.	2 mL
Medium coconut	½ cup	125 mL
Cut up gumdrop candies (no black)	½ cup	125 mL
Vanilla	½ tsp.	2 mL

Icing sugar, to coat

Cream butter and sugars well. Add eggs and beat.

Add flour, salt, rolled oats, baking powder, baking soda, coconut, gumdrops and vanilla. Mix together. Press in greased 9 x 9 inch (22 x 22 cm) pan. Bake in 350° (175°C) oven for 25 to 30 minutes.

Sift icing sugar over top when cool. Cuts into 36 squares.

Pictured on page 71.

CHERRY ALMOND SQUARES

This is a rich, crumbly, melt-in-your-mouth type square.

Butter (not margarine), softened	1 cup	250 mL
Brown sugar, packed	1 cup	250 mL
All-purpose flour	2 cups	500 mL
Finely cut candied cherries	½ cup	125 mL
Chopped blanched almonds	½ cup	125 mL
ICING		
Icing (confectioner's) sugar	1½ cups	375 mL
Butter or hard margarine, softened	3 tbsp.	50 mL
Cherry flavoring	½ tsp.	2 mL
Water	1½ tbsp.	25 mL

Combine butter, brown sugar and flour in a bowl. Knead together to make a ball of dough. Add cherries and almonds, squeezing in as best you can to distribute as evenly as possible. Press in ungreased 9 x 9 inch (22 x 22 cm) pan. Bake in 325°F (160°C) oven for 20 to 30 minutes until set and a golden brown. Cut while warm. Cool.

Icing: Beat all 4 ingredients in small bowl adding more liquid or icing sugar as needed so icing can be spread easily. Smooth over cooled squares which have already been cut while warm. Cuts into 36 squares.

Pictured on page 35.

QUICK HURRY BARS

These are the quickest of the quick.

Graham cracker crumbs	2 cups	500 mL
Flake coconut	1⅓ cups	325 mL
Chopped walnuts	1 cup	250 mL
Sweetened condensed milk	11 oz.	300 mL

Combine graham crumbs, coconut and walnuts in medium bowl. Add condensed milk and stir well. Scrape into well-greased 8 x 8 inch (20 x 20 cm) pan. Bake in 350°F (175°C) oven for 40 minutes or until wooden pick inserted in center comes out clean. Cool. Store, covered, airtight. Cuts into 25 squares.

Pictured on page 125.

CREAM CHEESE BROWNIES

These are fussy to layer before baking, but are worth the extra time it takes. Very attractive.

CHEESE LAYER		
Cream cheese, softened	4 oz.	125 g
Large egg	1	1
Granulated sugar	½ cup	125 mL
All-purpose flour	2 tbsp.	30 mL
Chopped maraschino cherries, well-drained	½ cup	125 mL
BROWNIE LAYER		
Large eggs	2	2
All-purpose flour	¾ cup	175 mL
Granulated sugar	1 cup	250 mL
Chopped walnuts	½ cup	125 mL
Salt	⅛ tsp.	0.5 mL
Cocoa	¼ cup	60 mL
Butter or hard margarine	½ cup	125 mL
ICING		
Icing (confectioner's) sugar	1⅓ cups	325 mL
Cocoa	⅓ cup	75 mL
Butter or hard margarine, softened	3 tbsp.	50 mL
Hot water or prepared coffee	1½ tbsp.	25 mL

Cheese Layer: Beat cream cheese and egg well. Blend sugar and flour in gradually, beating until blended. Stir in cherries. Set aside.

Brownie Layer: Beat eggs until frothy. Add next 4 ingredients. Mix.

Melt cocoa and butter in saucepan. Stir well. Add to egg mixture. Mix. Spread ⅔ of this mixture in greased 9 x 9 inch (22 x 22 cm) pan. Carefully put dabs of cream cheese filling here and there over top. Cover as completely as you can with remaining ⅓ brownie mixture by dropping half teaspoonfuls over top in rows. This will be patchy-looking but, when iced, they will look fine. Bake in 350°F (175°C) oven for 30 to 35 minutes. Should show signs of pulling away from edge of pan. Cool.

Icing: Put all 4 ingredients into small bowl. Beat. If too stiff to spread easily, add a few drops more liquid. If too runny, add more icing sugar. Spread over brownies. Cuts into 25 squares.

Pictured on page 35.

FRUIT COCKTAIL BARS

This is a very moist bar and it stays that way for days. May also be served hot with ice cream.

Large eggs	2	2
Granulated sugar	1½ cups	375 mL
Canned fruit cocktail, with juice	14 oz.	398 mL
All-purpose flour	2¼ cups	550 mL
Baking soda	2 tsp.	10 mL
Salt	½ tsp.	2 mL
Vanilla	1 tsp.	5 mL
Chopped walnuts	½ cup	125 mL
Brown sugar, packed	½ cup	125 mL
GLAZE		
Brown sugar, packed	¾ cup	175 mL
Vanilla	½ tsp.	2 mL
Butter or hard margarine	½ cup	125 mL
Milk	¼ cup	60 mL
Chopped walnuts (optional)	½ cup	125 mL

Beat eggs and sugar together well. Add fruit and juice. Stir to combine. Stir in flour, baking soda, salt and vanilla. Spread in greased 9 x 13 inch (22 x 33 cm) pan.

Sprinkle walnuts and brown sugar over batter in pan. Bake in 350°F (175°C) oven for 30 to 40 minutes or until set.

Glaze: Bring all 5 ingredients to a boil in a saucepan while stirring. Pour over warm bars. Cool. Cuts into 54 squares.

Pictured on page 35.

CHIP CRUMBLES

This is very quick and easy to make and has the flavor of chocolate chip cookies.

Butter or hard margarine, softened	1 cup	250 mL
Brown sugar, packed	1 cup	250 mL
Vanilla	1 tsp.	5 mL
All-purpose flour	2 cups	500 mL
Finely chopped walnuts	1 cup	250 mL
Semisweet chocolate chips	1 cup	250 mL

Crumble butter, brown sugar, vanilla and flour together in bowl. Stir in walnuts and chocolate chips. Pat in ungreased 9 x 9 inch (22 x 22 cm) pan. Bake in 350°F (175°C) oven for 25 minutes or until browned. Cut while still warm. Cool in pan. Cuts into 36 squares.

Pictured on page 71.

PEANUT BUTTER BARS

This is like shortbread with peanut butter flavor. Icing should not be omitted in these squares.

Butter or hard margarine, softened	1/2 cup	125 mL
Smooth peanut butter	1/4 cup	60 mL
Brown sugar, packed	3/4 cup	175 mL
Large egg	1	1
Vanilla	1 tsp.	5 mL
All-purpose flour	1 3/4 cups	425 mL
ICING		
Semisweet chocolate chips	2/3 cup	150 mL
Smooth peanut butter	3 tbsp.	50 mL

Mix all ingredients in bowl and pack in greased 9 x 9 inch (22 x 22 cm) pan. Bake in 350°F (175°C) oven for about 20 to 25 minutes. Cool.

Icing: Melt chocolate chips and peanut butter in saucepan over low heat. Stir. Spread on cooled bars. Cuts into 36 squares.

Pictured on page 71.

NEAPOLITAN SQUARES

A good keeper and an attractive addition to a plate of squares. Nicer to cut on the second or third day.

BOTTOM LAYER		
Butter or hard margarine	½ cup	125 mL
Graham cracker crumbs	1¼ cups	300 mL
Brown sugar, packed	½ cup	125 mL
All-purpose flour	⅓ cup	75 mL
SECOND LAYER		
Medium coconut	2 cups	450 mL
Sweetened condensed milk	11 oz.	300 mL
ICING		
Icing (confectioner's) sugar	2 cups	500 mL
Butter or hard margarine, softened	¼ cup	60 mL
Maraschino cherry juice (see Note)	3 tbsp.	50 mL

Bottom Layer: Melt butter in medium saucepan. Stir in graham crumbs, sugar and flour. Press in ungreased 9 x 9 inch (22 x 22 cm) pan. Bake in 350°F (175°C) oven for 10 minutes.

Second Layer: Combine coconut with condensed milk in another bowl. Do this just before spreading so the coconut doesn't have time to soak up the milk. It will spread more easily. Spread over bottom layer. Bake in 350°F (175°C) oven for 20 minutes or until a very slight tinge of light brown begins to show on the edges. Cool.

Icing: Beat icing sugar, butter and cherry juice together, adding a bit more juice, if needed to make icing soft enough to spread. Spread over cooled bars. Cover tightly and store at least a day to soften. Can be used the same day as baked but it is more difficult to cut. Cuts into 36 squares.

Note: If you do not have any cherry juice, use water with a bit of red food coloring with ¼ tsp. (1 mL) cherry or almond flavoring.

Pictured on cover.

CHOCOLATE WALNUT SLICE

A buttery fudge taste.

BOTTOM LAYER
Butter or hard margarine, softened	½ cup	125 mL
Brown sugar, packed	⅓ cup	75 mL
All-purpose flour	1¼ cups	300 mL
Salt	¼ tsp.	1 mL

SECOND LAYER
Large eggs	2	2
Brown sugar, packed	1 cup	250 mL
Cocoa	3 tbsp	50 mL
All-purpose flour	1 tbsp.	15 mL
Chopped walnuts	½ cup	125 mL
Medium coconut	1 cup	250 mL
Vanilla	1 tsp.	5 mL

ICING
Icing (confectioner's) sugar	1¼ cups	300 mL
Cocoa	⅓ cup	75 mL
Butter or hard margarine, softened	3 tbsp.	50 mL
Hot prepared coffee or water	1½ tbsp.	25 mL

Bottom Layer: Measure all 4 ingredients into bowl. Crumble together until mealy. Press in ungreased 9 × 9 inch (22 × 22 cm) pan. Set aside.

Second Layer: Beat eggs until foamy. Add rest of ingredients and stir well. Spread over bottom layer. Bake in 350°F (175°C) oven for 30 minutes. Cool.

Icing: Beat all 4 ingredients together in small bowl, adding more liquid or icing sugar if needed to spread easily. Spread over cooled bars. Cuts into 36 squares.

Pictured on page 71.

COCONUT GRAHAM CAKE

A one-step cake that, if left uniced, is not too sweet. It has a rich flavor.

Butter or hard margarine, softened	½ cup	125 mL
Large eggs	2	2
Granulated sugar	1 cup	250 mL
Vanilla	1 tsp.	5 mL
Graham cracker crumbs	2 cups	450 mL
All-purpose flour	3 tbsp.	50 mL
Baking powder	1 tsp.	5 mL
Salt	¼ tsp.	1 mL
Medium coconut	1 cup	250 mL
ICING		
Butter or hard margarine	¼ cup	60 mL
Brown sugar, packed	½ cup	125 mL
Milk	2 tbsp.	30 mL
Icing (confectioner's) sugar	1 cup	250 mL

Cream butter, eggs, sugar and vanilla. Add remaining ingredients, stirring well to blend. Pack in greased 9 x 9 inch (22 x 22 cm) pan. Bake in 350°F (175°C) oven for about 25 minutes or until a wooden pick inserted in center comes out clean. Cool.

Icing: Combine butter, brown sugar and milk in saucepan. Bring to a boil and simmer 2 minutes. Remove from heat. Cool.

Add icing sugar and beat. Add more milk if too stiff or more icing sugar if too thin. Spread over cake. Cuts into 36 squares.

Pictured on page 71.

APRICOT ZINGS

The bottom layer helps "make" this delicious square. It is even better when used the second day. A good seller at a bake sale.

BOTTOM LAYER
Butter or hard margarine	¾ cup	175 mL
Graham cracker crumbs	1 cup	250 mL
All-purpose flour	1 cup	250 mL
Brown sugar, packed	1 cup	250 mL
Medium coconut	½ cup	125 mL
Salt	½ tsp.	2 mL

FILLING
Dried apricots	1 cup	250 mL
Water to cover fruit		
Large eggs	2	2
Brown sugar, packed	1 cup	250 mL
Lemon juice, fresh or bottled	1 tbsp.	15 mL
All-purpose flour	⅓ cup	75 mL
Baking powder	½ tsp.	2 mL
Salt	¼ tsp.	1 mL

Bottom Layer: Melt butter in medium saucepan. Stir in next 5 ingredients until crumbly. Reserve 1 cup (250 mL). Pack the rest in ungreased 9 x 9 inch (22 x 22 cm) pan. Bake in 350°F (175°C) oven for 10 minutes.

Filling: Simmer apricots in water for 15 minutes. Drain and chop. Set aside.

Beat eggs until frothy. Add brown sugar and lemon juice. Mix. Measure flour, baking powder and salt into egg mixture. Stir. Add apricots and stir again. Spread over bottom layer. Sprinkle with reserved crumbs. Bake in 350°F (175°C) oven for 30 to 35 minutes. Cool. Cuts into 36 squares.

Pictured on page 143.

GRAHAM CRACKER CHEW

One of the fastest recipes going — that is once you get the dates cut up. When company is on the way, you can have this in the oven in no time. Cut it and eat it hot, plain, or with a dab of icing, which will run over the side as it melts.

Large eggs	2	2
Graham cracker crumbs	1½ cups	375 mL
Chopped walnuts	1 cup	250 mL
Chopped dates	1 cup	250 mL
Brown sugar, packed	1 cup	250 mL
Baking powder	1 tsp.	5 mL
ICING		
Butter or hard margarine, softened	3 tbsp.	50 mL
Icing (confectioner's) sugar	1½ cups	375 mL
Cocoa	⅓ cup	75 mL
Prepared coffee	1½ tbsp.	25 mL

Beat eggs in bowl until frothy. Add next 5 ingredients. Mix well with spoon. Press mixture in greased 9 x 9 inch (22 x 22 cm) pan. Bake in 350°F (175°C) oven for about 25 minutes. Cool.

Icing: Measure all 4 ingredients into bowl. Beat well, adding more coffee or icing sugar if required for spreading consistency. Spread over cooled squares. Cuts into 36 squares.

Pictured on page 125.

Having a big snack at bedtime won't count against your diet if you plan to sleep through breakfast.

CHOCOLATE DATE NUT SQUARES

This is really an outstanding chocolate square. Nice and moist.

Chopped dates	1 cup	250 mL
Baking soda	1 tsp.	5 mL
Boiling water	1½ cups	375 mL
Large eggs	2	2
Butter or hard margarine, softened	½ cup	125 mL
Granulated sugar	1 cup	250 mL
All-purpose flour	1½ cups	375 mL
Salt	¾ tsp.	4 mL
Baking soda	¾ tsp.	4 mL
TOPPING		
Brown sugar, packed	½ cup	125 mL
Chopped walnuts	½ cup	125 mL
Semisweet chocolate chips	1 cup	250 mL

Put dates and first amount of baking soda into large bowl. Pour boiling water over and stir. Set aside.

Beat eggs in another bowl. Stir in butter and sugar. Beat until well blended. Stir into date mixture. Measure flour, salt and second amount of baking soda into date mixture and stir together. Scrape into greased 9 x 13 inch (22 x 33 cm) pan. Batter will be thin and runny.

Topping: Stir brown sugar, walnuts and chocolate chips together in bowl. Sprinkle over batter in pan. Bake in 350°F (175°C) oven for 50 minutes or until a wooden pick inserted in center comes out clean. Cuts into 54 squares.

Pictured on page 71.

1. Lemon Graham Slice page 130
2. Bikini Bars page 133
3. Poppy Seed Squares page 150
4. Swirl Squares page 127
5. Ginger Bar page 122
6. Coconut Lemon Bars page 101
7. Apricot Chews page 141
8. Fruity Fruit Slice page 62
9. Peanut Butter Chip Squares page 146
10. Condensed Squares page 101
11. Black Bottom Slice page 51
12. Chinese Chews page 121
13. Marmalade Bars page 102
14. Banana Bars page 66
15. Raspberry Smacks page 117
16. Marshmallow Squares page 46

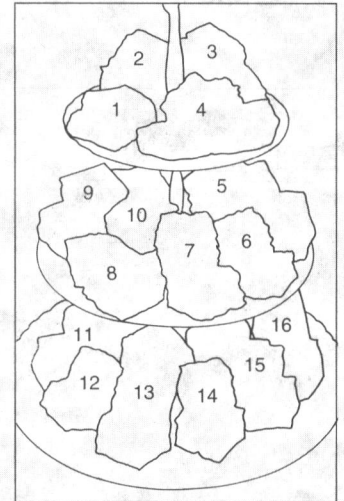

Tiered Tray Courtesy Of:
Eaton's China Dept.

Stained Glass Courtesy Of:
Winter Art Glass Studio, Inc.

ALMOND DATE SQUARES

Truly a delicious treat. Moist and a good keeper, these are good with or without the almonds.

BOTTOM LAYER		
Butter or hard margarine, softened	½ cup	125 mL
Granulated sugar	½ cup	125 mL
Egg yolks (large)	2	2
All-purpose flour	1½ cups	375 mL
Baking powder	1 tsp.	5 mL
Vanilla	1 tsp.	5 mL
FILLING		
Chopped dates	1 cup	250 mL
Water	½ cup	125 mL
TOP LAYER		
Egg whites (large)	2	2
Brown sugar, packed	1 cup	250 mL
Sliced or slivered almonds	3 tbsp.	50 mL

Bottom Layer: Mix all 6 ingredients well. Press in greased 9 x 9 inch (22 x 22 cm) pan. Set aside.

Filling: Boil dates and water together for 5 minutes. If mixture is too dry to spread easily, stir in a bit more water. Spread carefully over bottom layer.

Top Layer: Beat egg whites until frothy and turning white. Add brown sugar as you continue to beat until stiff. Spread over dates.

Sprinkle with almonds. Bake in 350°F (175°C) oven for 30 minutes. Cool. Cover to store. This gives the meringue a chance to soften. Cut with a clean sharp knife. Cuts into 36 squares.

Pictured on page 143.

Help yourself to someone else's candy. No calories here since they are the ones that shouldn't have bought them.

CHERRY SQUARES

This is one of the most popular bar-type cookies. After you've tried it you will understand why.

BOTTOM LAYER		
All-purpose flour	1¼ cups	300 mL
Brown sugar, packed	⅓ cup	75 mL
Butter or hard margarine, softened	½ cup	125 mL
SECOND LAYER		
Large eggs	2	2
Brown sugar, packed	1¼ cups	300 mL
All-purpose flour	1 tbsp.	15 mL
Baking powder	½ tsp.	2 mL
Salt	⅛ tsp.	0.5 mL
Medium coconut	1 cup	250 mL
Chopped walnuts	½ cup	125 mL
Candied or maraschino cherries, cut up	½ cup	125 mL
ICING		
Icing (confectioner's) sugar	1 cup	250 mL
Butter or hard margarine, softened	2 tbsp.	30 mL
Vanilla	½ tsp.	2 mL
Water or milk	1 tbsp.	15 mL

Bottom Layer: Crumble all 3 ingredients together well. Press in ungreased 9 x 9 inch (22 x 22 cm) pan. Bake in 350°F (175°C) oven for 15 minutes.

Second Layer: Beat eggs slightly and mix in the rest of the ingredients in order given. Spread over first layer. Return to oven and bake for 25 minutes until brown.

Icing: Beat all 4 ingredients together in small bowl, adding more water or icing sugar if needed to make a more spreadable mixture. Spread over cooled squares. This makes a minimum amount of icing. Cuts into 36 squares.

Pictured on page 71.

MOLASSES BARS

Add this to your list of squares that are not too sweet.

Butter or hard margarine, softened	½ cup	125 mL
Granulated sugar	½ cup	125 mL
Large egg, slightly beaten	1	1
Table molasses	¼ cup	60 mL
Salt	¼ tsp.	1 mL
Ground cinnamon	½ tsp.	2 mL
Ground ginger	¼ tsp.	1 mL
Ground cloves	¼ tsp.	1 mL
Hot prepared coffee	½ cup	125 mL
All-purpose flour	1¼ cups	300 mL
Baking soda	½ tsp.	2 mL
ICING		
Icing (confectioner's) sugar)	1½ cups	375 mL
Butter or hard margarine, softened	3 tbsp.	50 mL
Prepared orange juice	1½ tbsp.	25 mL

Cream butter and sugar together. Add egg. Add molasses, salt, cinnamon, ginger and cloves. Stir. Add ½ of prepared coffee and stir.

Mix flour and baking soda. Add ½ to creamed mixture and stir. Add the rest of coffee followed by rest of flour mixture, stirring after each addition. Spread in greased 9 x 9 inch (22 x 22 cm) pan. Bake in 350°F (175°C) oven for 20 to 25 minutes. A wooden pick inserted in center should come out clean.

Icing: Mix icing sugar, butter and orange juice in small bowl, adding more juice or icing sugar if needed. Spread over cooled bars. Cuts into 36 squares.

Pictured on page 107.

RASPBERRY BARS

Long thread coconut gives this a fancy, festive air. The red ribbon in the middle looks attractive among a tray of squares.

BOTTOM LAYER
All-purpose flour	1¼ cups	300 mL
Butter or hard margarine, softened	½ cup	125 mL
Granulated sugar	¼ cup	60 mL

FILLING
Raspberry jam (may use less)	1 cup	250 mL

TOP LAYER
Large eggs	2	2
Granulated sugar	1 cup	250 mL
Long thread coconut	2 cups	500 mL
Vanilla	1 tsp.	5 mL
Baking powder	½ tsp.	2 mL
All-purpose flour	1 tbsp.	15 mL

Bottom Layer: Combine all 3 ingredients in bowl. Mix well until crumbly. Press in ungreased 9 × 9 inch (22 × 22 cm) pan. Bake in 350°F (175°C) oven for 15 minutes.

Filling: Spoon jam in small dabs here and there over bottom layer. Spread carefully.

Top Layer: Beat eggs until frothy. Add sugar, coconut, vanilla, baking powder and flour. Stir to combine well. Spread over jam layer. Bake in 350° (175°C) oven for 25 to 35 minutes until golden brown. Cool. Cuts into 36 squares.

Pictured on page 71.

If you begin to feel nervous about eating all these squares, a good idea is to have the bathroom scale close to the sink counter so you can steady yourself while weighing by putting one hand on the counter.

DATE PECAN BARS

You can't tell by looking at this what it is going to taste like. It is the rum flavor that makes all the difference. Must be made a day or two ahead. Mmmm!

Chopped dates	1 cup	250 mL
Baking soda	1 tsp.	5 mL
Butter or hard margarine	½ cup	125 mL
Boiling water	¾ cup	175 mL
Dark rum (or 2 tsp., 10 mL, rum flavoring plus ¼ cup, 60 mL, water)	¼ cup	60 mL
Large egg	1	1
Granulated sugar	½ cup	125 mL
Vanilla	1 tsp.	5 mL
All-purpose flour	1½ cups	375 mL
Baking powder	1 tsp.	5 mL
TOPPING		
Brown sugar, packed	1 cup	250 mL
Butter or hard margarine, softened	3 tbsp.	50 mL
Cream	3 tbsp.	50 mL
Chopped pecans	1 cup	250 mL

Place dates into large mixing bowl. Sprinkle with baking soda and stir a bit to distribute. Add butter and boiling water. Continue to stir until butter has melted. Add rum. Stir and set aside.

Beat egg, sugar and vanilla together well in small bowl. Pour into date mixture.

Measure in flour and baking powder. Stir well. Spread in greased 9 x 9 inch (22 x 22 cm) pan. Bake in 350°F (175°C) oven for 25 minutes.

Topping: Mix first 2 ingredients together in bowl until crumbly.

Add cream and pecans. Mix. As soon as you take squares out of the oven, spread with topping and return to oven for 15 to 20 minutes until golden brown. Cool. Cover with tight plastic or foil and put on an out-of-the-way shelf in your cupboard so it can mellow for a day or two. Cuts into 36 squares.

Pictured on page 35.

CHOCOLATE ORANGE DROPS

Orange and chocolate are great go-togethers This is moist and a good keeper.

Butter or hard margarine, softened	½ cup	125 mL
Cream cheese, softened	4 oz.	125 g
Icing (confectioner's) sugar	½ cup	125 mL
Large egg	1	1
Grated orange rind	1 tbsp.	15 mL
Vanilla	1 tsp.	5 mL
All-purpose flour	1 cup	250 mL
Salt	½ tsp.	2 mL
Semisweet chocolate chips	1 cup	250 mL
ICING		
Cream cheese, softened	4 oz.	125 g
Frozen concentrated orange juice	3 tbsp.	50 mL
Icing (confectioner's) sugar	1½ cups	375 mL

Beat butter and cream cheese until light. Add icing sugar and egg. Beat until smooth. Add rind and vanilla. Stir. Mix in flour, salt and chocolate chips. Put into greased 9 x 9 inch (22 x 22 cm) pan. Bake in 350°F (175°C) oven for 25 to 30 minutes. Cool.

Icing: Beat cream cheese with orange juice. Add icing sugar and beat. Add more icing sugar or more orange juice as needed for easy spreading. Spread over bars. Keep refrigerated. Cut while cool. Allow to come to room temperature to soften before serving. Cuts into 36 squares.

Pictured on page 35.

The most perfect shape in the world is round. Have another sweet.

MERRY FRUIT BARS

A nice fruity and moist bar.

Large eggs	2	2
Granulated sugar	½ cup	125 mL
Vanilla	½ tsp.	2 mL
All-purpose flour	¾ cup	175 mL
Baking powder	¾ tsp.	4 mL
Salt	½ tsp.	2 mL
Cut mixed candied fruit	¾ cup	175 mL
Chopped dates	¼ cup	60 mL
Chopped walnuts	½ cup	125 mL

Beat eggs until thick and increased in volume. Add sugar and continue beating. Beat in vanilla. Add flour, baking powder, salt, fruit, dates and walnuts. Stir well. Pour into greased 8 x 8 inch (20 x 20 cm) pan. Bake in 350°F (175°C) oven for about 30 minutes until set. Cool. Wrap airtight to freeze. Cuts into 25 squares.

Pictured on page 35.

AUSTRALIAN HONEY BARS

A moist bar that is chewy.

Butter or hard margarine, softened	6 tbsp.	100 mL
Honey	½ cup	125 mL
Large eggs	3	3
All-purpose flour	1½ cups	375 mL
Baking powder	1 tsp.	5 mL
Raisins	1 cup	250 mL
Chopped walnuts	¾ cup	175 mL

Icing sugar, to cover

Cream butter and honey together. Add eggs 1 at a time, beating well after each addition. Stir in flour, baking powder, raisins and walnuts. Scrape into greased 9 x 9 inch (22 x 22 cm) pan. Bake in 350°F (175°C) oven for 30 minutes or until it firms.

Before serving, sift icing sugar over top. Cuts into 36 squares.

Pictured on page 125.

PRUNE CHIPS

You will never know how good prunes can taste until you try this.

Butter or hard margarine, softened	½ cup	125 mL
Large egg	1	1
Granulated sugar	1 cup	250 mL
Water	½ cup	125 mL
Lemon juice, fresh or bottled	2 tsp.	10 mL
Chopped walnuts	⅓ cup	75 mL
All-purpose flour	1½ cups	350 mL
Baking powder	½ tsp.	2 mL
Baking soda	½ tsp.	2 mL
Salt	½ tsp.	2 mL
Ground nutmeg	½ tsp.	2 mL
Ground cinnamon	½ tsp.	2 mL
Ground cloves	¼ tsp.	1 mL
Finely chopped dried pitted prunes	⅔ cup	150 mL

Beat butter, egg and sugar together until fluffy. Add water, lemon juice and walnuts. Beat well.

Combine flour, baking powder, baking soda, salt, nutmeg, cinnamon and cloves in another bowl. Add prunes. Stir to coat prunes. Add to egg mixture. Stir to combine. Pour into greased 9 × 9 inch (22 × 22 cm) pan. Bake in 350°F (175°C) oven for 40 to 50 minutes until a wooden pick inserted in center comes out clean. Cuts into 36 squares.

Pictured on page 35.

The trouble with big-hearted cooks is that their hips are usually the same size.

CHOCOLATE FRUIT SQUARES

A chocolate fruity bar that stays moist for days.

BOTTOM LAYER		
Butter or hard margarine, softened	½ cup	125 mL
Cocoa	¼ cup	60 mL
All-purpose flour	1 cup	250 mL
Granulated sugar	¼ cup	60 mL

SECOND LAYER		
Large eggs	2	2
Chopped dates	¾ cup	175 mL
Chopped candied cherries	¾ cup	175 mL
All-purpose flour	1 tbsp.	15 mL
Vanilla	½ tsp.	2 mL
Lemon juice, fresh or bottled	1 tsp.	5 mL

ICING		
Icing (confectioner's) sugar	1½ cups	375 mL
Butter or hard margarine, softened	3 tbsp.	50 mL
Vanilla	½ tsp.	2 mL
Water or milk	1½ tbsp.	25 mL

Bottom Layer: Crumble all 4 ingredients together in bowl. Press in ungreased 9 x 9 inch (22 x 22 cm) pan. Bake in 350°F (175°C) oven for about 10 minutes.

Second Layer: Beat eggs slightly. Stir in dates, cherries, flour, vanilla and lemon juice. Mix well and spoon over bottom layer. Bake in 350°F (175°C) oven for 20 to 25 minutes. Cool.

Icing: Beat icing sugar, butter, vanilla and water in small bowl. Adjust to spreading consistency with more icing sugar or more water. Spread over cooled fruit squares. Cut when set. Cuts into 36 squares.

Pictured on page 35.

TWEED SQUARES

Now here is a really different look.

Butter or hard margarine, softened	½ cup	125 mL
Granulated sugar	⅔ cup	150 mL
All-purpose flour	1⅓ cups	325 mL
Baking powder	2 tsp.	10 mL
Salt	½ tsp.	2 mL
Milk	½ cup	125 mL
Egg whites (large)	2	2
Semisweet chocolate baking squares, grated	2 × 1 oz.	2 × 28 g
ICING		
Icing (confectioner's) sugar	1½ cups	375 mL
Butter or hard margarine, softened	3 tbsp.	50 mL
Vanilla	½ tsp.	2 mL
Water	1½ tbsp.	25 mL
Semisweet chocolate baking squares, cut up	2 × 1 oz.	2 × 28 g
Butter or hard margarine	1 tbsp.	15 mL
Grated paraffin wax	2 tsp.	10 mL

Cream butter and sugar until blended. Combine flour, baking powder and salt. Add flour mixture and milk alternately to creamed mixture. Beat egg whites in separate bowl until stiff. Fold into batter. Fold in grated chocolate. Pour into greased 9 × 9 inch (22 × 22 cm) pan. Bake in 350°F (175°C) oven for about 35 minutes. Cool.

Icing: Beat first 4 ingredients together in bowl, adjusting water or icing sugar as needed to make proper spreading consistency. Spread over cooled squares. Let stand at least 1 hour.

Melt next 3 ingredients in saucepan over low heat. Wax is to give chocolate some shine and to make it thinner. It can be omitted if desired. Spread over white icing. Allow to set before cutting. Cuts into 36 squares.

Pictured on page 71.

COCONUT LEMON BARS

For both a caramel and a lemon flavor, this is a winner. Richer than other lemon bars.

BOTTOM LAYER
Butter or hard margarine, softened	½ cup	125 mL
Brown sugar, packed	½ cup	125 mL
All-purpose flour	1 cup	250 mL

SECOND LAYER
Large eggs	2	2
Brown sugar, packed	1 cup	250 mL
Lemon juice, fresh or bottled	2 tbsp.	30 mL
Grated lemon rind	1 tsp.	5 mL
Salt	¼ tsp.	1 mL
Chopped walnuts	1 cup	250 mL
Coarsely chopped raisins	½ cup	125 mL
Medium coconut	1 cup	250 mL

Bottom Layer: Mix all 3 ingredients together until mealy. Press in ungreased 9 x 9 inch (22 x 22 cm) pan. Bake in 350°F (175°C) oven for about 10 minutes.

Second Layer: Beat eggs until frothy. Add rest of ingredients. Stir to mix. Pour over bottom layer. Bake in 350°F (175°C) oven for about 25 minutes or until golden brown. Cut while slightly warm. Cuts into 36 squares.

Pictured on page 89.

CONDENSED SQUARES

Condensed in more ways than one, especially in time needed to prepare for the oven.

Graham cracker crumbs	1½ cups	375 mL
Chopped walnuts	1 cup	250 mL
Flake coconut	1½ cups	375 mL
Cocoa	⅓ cup	75 mL
Vanilla	1 tsp.	5 mL
Sweetened condensed milk	11 oz.	300 mL

Combine all ingredients in bowl. Mix well. Pack in greased 8 x 8 inch (20 x 20 cm) pan. Bake in 350°F (175°C) oven for 30 to 35 minutes. Store covered. Cuts into 25 squares.

Pictured on page 89.

MARMALADE BARS

A tasty bar made with marmalade.

All-purpose flour	2 cups	500 mL
Brown sugar, packed	¾ cup	175 mL
Butter or hard margarine, softened	¾ cup	175 mL
Salt	⅛ tsp.	0.5 mL
Grated orange rind	¼ cup	60 mL
Large egg, beaten	1	1
FILLING		
Orange marmalade (or other flavor)	1 cup	250 mL
Reserved crumb mixture		
ICING		
Icing (confectioner's) sugar	1½ cups	375 mL
Butter or hard margarine, softened	3 tbsp.	50 mL
Orange marmalade	2 tbsp.	30 mL
Orange flavoring	¼ tsp.	1 mL

Crumble first 6 ingredients together well. Press about ⅔ of the mixture in ungreased 9 x 9 inch (22 x 22 cm) pan.

Filling: Drop little dabs of marmalade here and there over surface. Spread. Sprinkle with remaining crumbs. Press down slightly with your hand. Bake in 350°F (175°C) oven for 25 minutes or until golden brown. Cool.

Icing: Beat all 4 ingredients together in bowl. Add a bit of water or icing sugar if needed for easy spreading. Spread over cooled bars. Let set. Cuts into 36 squares.

Pictured on page 89.

RAISIN SQUARES

For a not-too-sweet square, this is a good choice.

Water	½ cup	125 mL
Raisins	1 cup	250 mL
Baking soda	1 tsp.	5 mL
Butter or hard margarine, softened	½ cup	125 mL
Granulated sugar	⅔ cup	150 mL
Large egg	1	1
Vanilla	1 tsp.	5 mL
All-purpose flour	1⅓ cups	325 mL
Baking powder	1 tsp.	5 mL
Salt	⅛ tsp.	0.5 mL

Icing (confectioner's) sugar, to cover

Bring water and raisins to a boil in saucepan. Remove from heat and stir in baking soda. Cool.

Cream butter with sugar in mixing bowl. Add egg and vanilla. Beat. Stir in raisin mixture.

Measure in flour, baking powder and salt. Mix and spread in greased 9 x 9 inch (22 x 22 cm) pan. Bake in 350°F (175°C) oven for 35 to 40 minutes.

Sift icing sugar over top when cool, if an added touch is required. Cuts into 36 squares.

Pictured on page 125.

BAKED FRUIT ROLL

A very different touch. You do the shaping after the baking.

Large eggs	2	2
Granulated sugar	1 cup	250 mL
Chopped dates	1 cup	250 mL
Chopped walnuts	1 cup	250 mL
Medium coconut	1 cup	250 mL
Vanilla	1 tsp.	5 mL
Almond flavoring	¼ tsp.	1 mL

Granulated sugar, to coat

Beat eggs in medium bowl until frothy. Add sugar slowly, while beating. Beat until fluffy.

Add dates, walnuts, coconut, vanilla and almond flavoring. Mix well. Pour into ungreased 2 quart (2 L) casserole. Bake in 350°F (175°C) oven for 30 minutes.

Stir occasionally, scraping down sides, until cool enough to handle. Form into a roll about 2 inches (5 cm) or more in diameter. Coat with sugar. Chill. Slice as needed.

Pictured on page 107.

PINEAPPLE FILLED BARS

There is a thick layer of pineapple which gives this its flavor and helps to keep it moist.

BOTTOM LAYER		
Brown sugar, packed	1 cup	250 mL
All-purpose flour	1 cup	250 mL
Butter or hard margarine, softened	½ cup	125 mL
Salt	⅛ tsp.	0.5 mL
Medium coconut	1½ cups	350 mL
FILLING		
Granulated sugar	¾ cup	175 mL
Lemon juice, fresh or bottled	1 tbsp.	15 mL
Crushed pineapple, with juice	1 cup	250 mL
Butter or hard margarine	1 tbsp.	15 mL
Cornstarch	3 tbsp.	50 mL
Reserved crumb mixture		

Bottom Layer: Mix all 5 ingredients until crumbly. Spread about ⅔ in greased 9 x 9 inch (22 x 22 cm) pan. Set aside.

Filling: Stir next 5 ingredients together in saucepan. Bring to a boil while stirring over medium heat. Cool slightly. Spread over bottom layer. Cover with remaining crumbs pressing down with your hand. Bake in 350°F (175°C) oven for 25 minutes or until golden brown in color. Cut while warm into 36 squares.

Pictured on page 35.

EASY GRAHAM BARS

This is another quick and easy square.

Graham cracker crumbs	3 cups	750 mL
Evaporated milk	1 cup	250 mL
Granulated sugar	1 cup	250 mL
Butter or hard margarine, softened	¼ cup	60 mL
Vanilla	1 tsp.	5 mL
Chopped walnuts	1 cup	250 mL
Semisweet chocolate chips	1 cup	250 mL

Measure all ingredients into bowl. Mix well. Spread in greased 9 x 9 inch (22 x 22 cm) pan. Bake in 350°F (175°C) oven for 35 minutes or until set. Cool. Cuts into 36 squares.

Pictured on page 125.

ORANGE SQUARES

You will need a food grinder or processor for this one. It isn't the same without it.

Medium orange	1	1
Raisins	1 cup	250 mL
Butter or hard margarine, softened	½ cup	125 mL
Granulated sugar	1 cup	250 mL
Large egg	1	1
All-purpose flour	2 cups	500 mL
Baking powder	½ tsp.	2 mL
Salt	¼ tsp.	1 mL
GLAZE		
Reserved orange juice	2 tbsp.	30 mL
Icing (confectioner's) sugar	1½ cups	375 mL

Cut unpeeled orange into quarters. Squeeze 2 tbsp. (30 mL) of juice into cup and set aside for glaze. Put orange pieces (with peel) and raisins through food grinder.

Cream butter and sugar together. Add egg and beat well. Add flour, baking powder and salt. Stir in raisin mixture. Batter will be stiff. Press in greased 9 x 13 inch (22 x 33 cm) pan. Bake in 350°F (175°C) oven for about 25 minutes.

Glaze: Mix orange juice and icing sugar well, adding more icing sugar or orange juice to make a barely pourable glaze. Spread on squares that are still warm. Allow to set before cutting. Cuts into 54 squares.

Pictured on page 143.

Any tidbits eaten in the dark are quite safe. After all, your body can't see what it's doing.

POTATO CHIP BARS

Potato chips make this a favorite for kids

Butter, softened	½ cup	125 mL
Butter or hard margarine, softened	½ cup	125 mL
Granulated sugar	½ cup	125 mL
Vanilla	1 tsp.	5 mL
All-purpose flour	2 cups	500 mL
Well-crushed potato chips	1 cup	250 mL
Finely chopped walnuts	½ cup	125 mL

Cream butter, margarine and sugar. Add vanilla and flour. Mix until it forms a ball. Work in potato chips and nuts. Pat in greased 9 x 9 inch (22 x 22 cm) pan. Bake in 350°F (175°C) oven for 15 to 20 minutes. Cut before cooled too much. Cuts into 36 squares.

Pictured on page 35.

1. Mystery Cake page 148
2. Cinnamon Bars page 132
3. Molasses Bars page 93
4. Chocolate Chip Squares page 123
5. Lemon Crunch page 60
6. Magic Bars page 124
7. Baked Fruit Roll page 103
8. Chocolate Smacks page 147
9. Chocolate Coconut Melts page 130
10. Butterscotch Toffee Bars page 134
11. Lemon Mardi Gras page 139
12. Sesame Squares page 137
13. Raisin Spice Bars page 149
14. Orange Coconut Chew page 114
15. Almond Bars page 151
16. Caramel Shortbread page 131
17. Brownies page 136
18. Caramel Toffee Squares page 135.

Trays Courtesy Of:
The Enchanted Kitchen

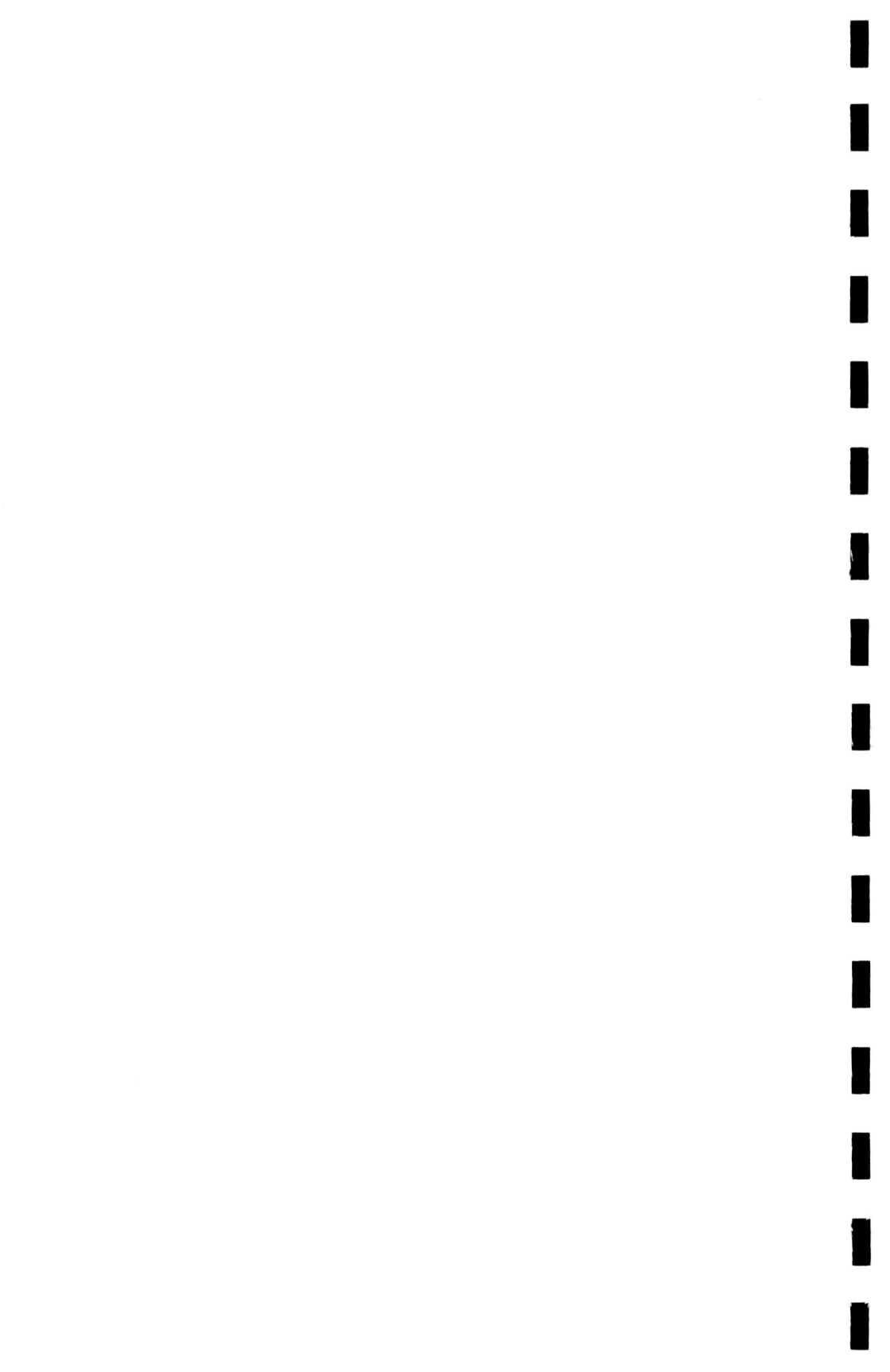

FRIEDA'S NUMBER 89

A cranberry spice bar that tastes like your favorite apple spice pudding. It freezes really well and only needs ten minutes thawing time. Excellent!

Butter or hard margarine, softened	¼ cup	60 mL
Brown sugar, packed	½ cup	125 mL
Granulated sugar	½ cup	125 mL
Large egg	1	1
Vanilla	1 tsp.	5 mL
Sour cream	¼ cup	60 mL
All-purpose flour	1 cup	250 mL
Baking powder	1 tsp.	5 mL
Salt	¼ tsp.	1 mL
Ground cinnamon	¼ tsp.	1 mL
Coarsely chopped cranberries, fresh or frozen	½ cup	125 mL
Chopped walnuts	½ cup	125 mL
Peeled, cored and coarsely chopped apple	½ cup	125 mL
TOPPING		
Granulated sugar	1 tbsp.	15 mL
Ground cinnamon	½ tsp.	2 mL

Beat butter, sugars and egg together in medium bowl. Add vanilla and sour cream. Mix. Stir in flour, baking powder, salt and cinnamon. Add cranberries, walnuts and apple. Mix well. Spread in greased 9 x 9 inch (22 x 22 cm) pan.

Topping: Mix sugar and cinnamon in small bowl. Sprinkle over batter in pan. Bake in 350°F (175°C) oven for 30 minutes. A wooden pick inserted in the center should come out clean. Cuts into 36 squares.

Pictured on page 125.

CHEWY NUT BARS

These have a caramel flavor combined with the chocolate of the chips. Chewy.

Butter or hard margarine	½ cup	125 mL
Brown sugar, packed	1 cup	250 mL
Vanilla	½ tsp.	2 mL
Large egg	1	1
All-purpose flour	1¼ cups	300 mL
Baking powder	1 tsp.	5 mL
Salt	¼ tsp.	1 mL
Finely chopped walnuts	¼ cup	60 mL
Semisweet chocolate chips	½ cup	125 mL
ICING		
Butter or hard margarine	3 tbsp.	50 mL
Brown sugar, packed	⅓ cup	75 mL
Milk	1½ tbsp.	25 mL
Icing (confectioner's) sugar	1 cup	250 mL

Melt butter in large saucepan. Remove from heat. Stir in brown sugar and vanilla. Add egg. Beat until well blended.

Measure in flour, baking powder and salt. Stir. Scrape into greased 8 x 8 inch (20 x 20 cm) pan.

Sprinkle walnuts and chocolate chips over top. Press with hand to ensure they stick. Bake in 350°F (175°C) oven for 30 to 40 minutes until set in center. Cool.

Icing: Put butter, brown sugar and milk in saucepan. Bring to boil and simmer 2 minutes. Cool. Stir in icing sugar. Add more icing sugar, if needed to thicken, or add more milk if too thick for easy spreading. Smooth over squares. Cuts into 25 squares.

Pictured on page 143.

THREE LAYER SLICE

The top layer completes this square by forming an icing or a topping. Nothing more is needed after baking.

BOTTOM LAYER
All-purpose flour	2 cups	500 mL
Butter or hard margarine, softened	½ cup	125 mL
Granulated sugar	3 tbsp.	50 mL
Salt	½ tsp.	2 mL

SECOND LAYER
Brown sugar, packed	1 cup	250 mL
Butter or hard margarine, softened	¼ cup	60 mL
Egg yolks (large)	3	3
Milk	½ cup	125 mL
Vanilla	1 tsp.	5 mL
Raisins	1 cup	250 mL
All-purpose flour	¾ cup	175 mL
Baking powder	1 tbsp.	15 mL

TOP LAYER
Brown sugar, packed	1 cup	250 mL
Egg whites (large)	3	3
Medium coconut	1 cup	250 mL
Vanilla	1 tsp.	5 mL

Bottom Layer: Crumble all 4 ingredients in bowl. Press firmly in ungreased 9 x 13 inch (22 x 33 cm) pan. Bake in 350°F (175°C) oven for 10 minutes.

Second Layer: Measure next 8 ingredients into bowl. Mix well. Pour over first layer. Continue to bake for 20 to 25 minutes.

Top Layer: Measure last 4 ingredients into bowl. Stir. Spread over second layer. Return to oven for about 15 minutes more. Cool. Cuts into 54 squares.

Pictured on page 125.

NUTTED GUMDROPS

It is usually a surprise to find out that the fruit is candy.

Evaporated milk	¾ cup	175 mL
Finely chopped gumdrops (no black)	1 cup	250 mL
Butter or hard margarine, softened	½ cup	125 mL
Granulated sugar	½ cup	125 mL
Large egg	1	1
Vanilla	1 tsp.	5 mL
All-purpose flour	1 cup	250 mL
Baking powder	1 tsp.	5 mL
Salt	½ tsp.	2 mL
Chopped walnuts	½ cup	125 mL
ICING		
Icing (confectioner's) sugar	1½ cups	375 mL
Butter or hard margarine, softened	2 tbsp.	30 mL
Evaporated milk	1½ tbsp.	25 mL
Vanilla	½ tsp.	2 mL

In small bowl combine milk with gumdrops. Let stand for 15 minutes.

In another bowl beat together butter, sugar, egg and vanilla. Add milk mixture. Stir.

Measure in flour, baking powder, salt and walnuts. Stir well. Spread in greased 9 x 9 inch (22 x 22 cm) pan. Bake in 350°F (175°C) oven for 25 to 30 minutes. Cool slightly.

Icing: Beat all 4 ingredients together until smooth. Add more liquid or icing sugar if needed to make proper spreading consistency. Spread over lukewarm squares. Cuts into 36 squares.

Pictured on page 125.

CRANBERRY SQUARES

A pretty square. It tastes as good as it looks. Nice and chewy.

BOTTOM LAYER
All-purpose flour	1½ cups	375 mL
Brown sugar, packed	½ cup	125 mL
Butter or hard margarine, softened	½ cup	125 mL
Salt	⅛ tsp.	0.5 mL

SECOND LAYER
Large eggs	2	2
Granulated sugar	1 cup	250 mL
Salt	¼ tsp.	1 mL
All-purpose flour	⅓ cup	75 mL
Baking powder	1 tsp.	5 mL
Raisins, chopped a bit	½ cup	125 mL
Medium coconut	½ cup	125 mL
Whole cranberry sauce, drained slightly	¾ cup	175 mL

ICING
Icing (confectioner's) sugar	1½ cups	375 mL
Butter or hard margarine	3 tbsp.	50 mL
Water or milk	1½ tbsp.	25 mL
Vanilla	½ tsp.	2 mL

Bottom Layer: Measure all 4 ingredients into large bowl. Mix until crumbly. Press in ungreased 8 × 8 inch (20 × 20 cm) pan. Bake in 350°F (175°C) oven for 10 minutes.

Second Layer: Beat eggs in same bowl. Add remaining ingredients. Mix well. Spread over bottom layer. Bake in 350°F (175°C) oven for 25 to 35 minutes until firm in center.

Icing: Beat all 4 ingredients together in small bowl adding more liquid or icing sugar if needed for easy spreading. Spread over cooled bars. Cuts into 25 squares.

Pictured on page 125.

ORANGE COCONUT CHEWS

A chewy moist square with just a hint of orange.

Butter or hard margarine	½ cup	125 mL
Brown sugar, packed	1 cup	250 mL
Large egg	1	1
Vanilla	1 tsp.	5 mL
Grated orange rind	2 tsp.	10 mL
All-purpose flour	½ cup	125 mL
Salt	½ tsp.	2 mL
Baking powder	1 tsp.	5 mL
Medium coconut	1 cup	250 mL
Chopped dates	1 cup	250 mL
ICING		
Icing (confectioner's) sugar	1½ cups	375 mL
Butter or hard margarine, softened	2 tbsp.	30 mL
Frozen concentrated orange juice	1½ tbsp.	25 mL

Melt butter in large saucepan. Remove from heat and mix in brown sugar, egg, vanilla and orange rind. Add flour, salt, baking powder, coconut and dates. Stir well. Pack in greased 8 x 8 inch (20 x 20 cm) pan. Bake in 350°F (175°C) oven for about 30 minutes. An inserted wooden pick should come out clean. Cool.

Icing: Beat all 3 ingredients together in bowl. If icing is too soft add more icing sugar or if too firm add more juice, a wee bit at a time. Spread over chews. Cuts into 25 squares.

Pictured on page 107.

Go ahead and eat all those goodies. No point in looking like a dream. You will just give someone insomnia!

CHEWY CANDY BARS

For an extra rich treat, this chewy square fills the bill.

BOTTOM LAYER		
Butter or hard margarine, softened	½ cup	125 mL
Brown sugar, packed	1 cup	250 mL
Large egg	1	1
Vanilla	½ tsp.	2 mL
All-purpose flour	¾ cup	175 mL
Baking soda	½ tsp.	2 mL
Salt	½ tsp.	2 mL
Quick-cooking rolled oats	1 cup	250 mL
SECOND LAYER		
Sweetened condensed milk	⅔ cup	150 mL
Cream cheese, softened	4 oz.	125 g
Vanilla	½ tsp.	2 mL
Finely chopped walnuts	½ cup	125 mL
ICING		
Reserved milk mixture	3 tbsp.	50 mL
Semisweet chocolate chips	⅓ cup	75 mL
Milk, as needed		

Bottom Layer: Beat together butter, brown sugar, egg and vanilla in a bowl. Add flour, baking soda, salt and rolled oats. Mix well. Pack in greased 9 x 9 inch (22 x 22 cm) pan. Set aside.

Second Layer: Beat condensed milk, cream cheese and vanilla together. Reserve 3 tbsp. (50 mL) for icing. Spread remainder over bottom layer.

Sprinkle walnuts over top. Bake in 350°F (175°C) oven for 25 minutes until set.

Icing: Place the milk mixture and chocolate chips together in small saucepan and melt over low heat. Add some milk, 1 tsp. (5 mL) at a time, until mixture will pour from spoon in a drizzle. Drizzle or spread icing over hot bars as soon as they come from the oven. Cool. Cuts into 36 squares.

Pictured on page 125.

LEMON SQUARES

A simple recipe. Lemon lovers can easily vary the amount of lemon juice that is added.

BOTTOM LAYER

All-purpose flour	1½ cups	375 mL
Granulated sugar	¼ cup	60 mL
Butter or hard margarine, softened	½ cup	125 mL

SECOND LAYER

Large eggs	2	2
Lemon juice, fresh or bottled	3 tbsp.	50 mL
Granulated sugar	1 cup	250 mL
All-purpose flour	2 tbsp.	30 mL
Baking powder	½ tsp.	2 mL
Medium coconut	1 cup	250 mL
Salt	¼ tsp.	1 mL

ICING

Icing (confectioner's) sugar	1½ cups	375 mL
Butter or hard margarine, softened	2 tbsp.	30 mL
Lemon juice, fresh or bottled	4 tsp.	20 mL

Bottom Layer: Crumble all 3 ingredients until mealy. Press in ungreased 9 x 9 inch (22 x 22 cm) pan. Bake in 350°F (175°C) oven for 15 to 20 minutes.

Second Layer: Beat eggs slightly. Stir in next 6 ingredients. Spread over first layer. Bake in 350°F (175°C) oven for 30 minutes until set in center and light brown in color. Cool.

Icing: Combine icing sugar, butter and lemon juice in small bowl. Beat well, adding more lemon juice a bit at a time as needed for easy spreading. Spread over cooled bars. Allow to set. Cuts into 36 squares.

Pictured on page 143.

RASPBERRY SMACKS

A rich, sticky square for special company. Best eaten fresh.

BOTTOM LAYER
All-purpose flour	1½ cups	375 mL
Brown sugar, packed	½ cup	125 mL
Butter or hard margarine, softened	½ cup	125 mL
Baking powder	1 tsp.	5 mL
Salt	¼ tsp.	1 mL
Egg yolks (large)	2	2
Vanilla	1 tsp.	5 mL

FILLING
Raspberry jam	1 cup	250 mL

TOP LAYER
Egg whites (large), room temperature	2	2
Brown sugar, packed	1 cup	250 mL
Chopped walnuts (optional)	½ cup	125 mL

Bottom Layer: Crumble all 7 ingredients together until mealy. Press in ungreased 9 x 9 inch (22 x 22 cm) pan.

Filling: Drop jam in small dabs over bottom layer. Spread carefully.

Top Layer: Beat egg whites until frothy. Add brown sugar ⅓ at a time, beating until stiff. Add walnuts if you plan to use them. Spoon over jam layer. Bake in 350°F (175°C) oven for 25 minutes until golden. When cool, cut with sharp knife dipped in hot water, between each cut. Cuts into 36 squares.

Pictured on page 89.

Paré Pointer

Anything consumed while suffering a cold doesn't count. If you can't taste it you can't absorb it.

ORANGE DATE BARS

The dates keep these moist as well as lending their special flavor.

Butter or hard margarine, melted	½ cup	125 mL
Granulated sugar	½ cup	125 mL
Grated orange rind	1 tsp.	5 mL
Prepared orange juice	3 tbsp.	50 mL
Large egg	1	1
All-purpose flour	1 cup	250 mL
Baking soda	½ tsp.	2 mL
Chopped walnuts	½ cup	125 mL
Chopped dates	½ cup	125 mL
ICING		
Icing (confectioner's) sugar	1½ cups	375 mL
Butter or hard margarine, softened	2 tbsp.	30 mL
Grated orange rind (optional)	1 tsp.	5 mL
Prepared orange juice	1½ tbsp.	25 mL

Combine butter with sugar, orange rind and first amount of orange juice in bowl. Blend well. Add egg and beat.

Mix flour and baking soda in separate bowl. Stir into batter.

Add walnuts and dates. Stir to mix. Spread in greased 9 x 9 inch (22 x 22 cm) pan. Bake in 350°F (175°C) oven for 20 to 25 minutes, being careful not to overbake. Cool.

Icing: Beat all 4 ingredients together in bowl. Add more orange juice or icing sugar if needed for easy spreading. Spread over cooled bars. Cuts into 36 squares.

Pictured on page 125.

Healthy size snacks taken at bedtime are really medication. Would you rather live on sleeping pills? Calorie count of zero.

GRANT'S SPECIAL

Otherwise known as Seafoam Chews. His friend's mother made this "really good square" so what else could I do?

BOTTOM LAYER
Butter or hard margarine, softened	½ cup	125 mL
Granulated sugar	½ cup	125 mL
Brown sugar, packed	½ cup	125 mL
All-purpose flour	2 cups	500 mL
Baking powder	2 tsp.	10 mL
Baking soda	1 tsp.	5 mL
Salt	½ tsp.	2 mL
Egg yolks (large)	2	2
Milk	3 tbsp.	50 mL
Vanilla	1 tsp.	5 mL

SECOND LAYER
Semisweet chocolate chips	1 cup	250 mL

THIRD LAYER
Egg whites (large), room temperature	2	2
Brown sugar, packed	1 cup	250 mL

TOP LAYER
Chopped salted peanuts	¾ cup	175 mL

Bottom Layer: Measure all 10 ingredients into large bowl. Crumble together well. Press in ungreased 9 x 9 inch (22 x 22 cm) pan at least 2 inches (5 cm) deep. This is a higher square than most.

Second Layer: Sprinkle chocolate chips evenly over bottom layer.

Third Layer: Beat egg whites until frothy. Add brown sugar ⅓ at a time, beating until stiff. Spread carefully over chocolate chips.

Top Layer: Sprinkle peanuts over beaten egg white, pressing lightly as they tend to fall off when baked. Bake in 350°F (175°C) oven for 35 minutes. Cool. Cover to soften meringue for easier cutting. Cuts into 36 squares.

Pictured on page 125.

LEMON CRUMB SQUARES

The cracker crumbs in the bottom layer give this a different twist. It is excellent even though it takes a bit more time than some others to prepare.

BOTTOM LAYER
Butter or hard margarine	¾ cup	175 mL
Graham cracker crumbs	1¾ cups	425 mL
Granulated sugar	½ cup	125 mL
All-purpose flour	¾ cup	175 mL
Medium coconut	½ cup	125 mL

FILLING
Granulated sugar	½ cup	125 mL
Large egg	1	1
Lemon, grated rind and juice	1	1
Fine coconut	½ cup	125 mL

Reserved crumb mixture

Bottom Layer: Melt butter in medium saucepan. Stir in graham crumbs, sugar, flour and coconut. Press just over ½ of mixture in ungreased 9 x 9 inch (22 x 22 cm) pan. Set aside.

Filling: In double boiler put sugar, egg, lemon rind, lemon juice and coconut. Cook and stir over boiling water until thickened. Pour filling over bottom layer.

Spread reserved crumbs over filling. Press slightly with hand. Bake in 350°F (175°C) oven for 25 to 30 minutes until set. Cool. Cuts into 36 squares.

Pictured on page 125.

Did you know that sampling a square or two before company comes (to see if it is right to serve), doesn't count on your diet?

CHINESE CHEWS

Tradition has it that each "chew" be rolled in icing sugar. It is just as good with the sugar sifted over top, thereby saving all that individual handling. This recipe uses white sugar instead of brown sugar.

Granulated sugar	1 cup	250 mL
Chopped dates	1 cup	250 mL
Baking powder	1 tsp.	5 mL
Salt	¼ tsp.	1 mL
Chopped walnuts	½ cup	125 mL
All-purpose flour	¾ cup	175 mL
Large eggs	2	2
Icing (confectioner's) sugar, to cover		

Mix first 6 ingredients in bowl.

Beat eggs in small bowl until light and thickened. Pour over dry mixture and stir until well moistened. Scrape batter into greased 9 x 9 inch (22 x 22 cm) pan. Bake in 350°F (175°C) oven for about 25 minutes. An inserted wooden pick should come out clean.

Cut into small squares and roll in icing sugar while still warm, or cool and sift icing sugar over top. Cuts into 36 squares.

Pictured on page 89.

Paré Pointer

If you are on an expense account, you must order extra desserts while you have the chance. They are tax deductions, not diet wreckers.

GINGER BAR

One of the few squares that has this flavor. Try them. Not a speck of ginger in them!

Butter or hard margarine, softened	½ cup	125 mL
Brown sugar, packed	½ cup	125 mL
Large egg	1	1
Mild molasses	½ cup	125 mL
Milk	½ cup	125 mL
Coarsely chopped raisins	½ cup	125 mL
Vanilla	½ tsp.	2 mL
All-purpose flour	2 cups	500 mL
Salt	¼ tsp.	1 mL
Baking powder	1½ tsp.	7 mL
Chopped walnuts	½ cup	125 mL
ICING		
Icing (confectioner's) sugar	1½ cups	375 mL
Butter or hard margarine, softened	3 tbsp.	50 mL
Vanilla	½ tsp.	2 mL
Water or milk	1½ tbsp.	25 mL

Beat butter, brown sugar and egg in bowl. Add molasses and stir. Stir in remaining ingredients. Spread in greased 9 x 9 inch (22 x 22 cm) pan. Bake in 350°F (175°C) oven for about 30 minutes until a wooden pick inserted near the center comes out clean.

Icing: Beat icing sugar, butter, vanilla and water, adding a bit more liquid or icing sugar if needed for proper spreading consistency. Spread over warm bars. Let set. Cuts into 36 squares.

Pictured on page 89.

CHOCOLATE CHIP SQUARES

This is a moist, caramel-tasting square, with the chocolate flavor giving it the extra touch.

Butter or hard margarine, softened	½ cup	125 mL
Brown sugar, packed	½ cup	125 mL
Granulated sugar	¼ cup	60 mL
Large egg	1	1
Vanilla	1 tsp.	5 mL
All-purpose flour	1 cup	250 mL
Baking soda	½ tsp.	2 mL
Salt	½ tsp.	2 mL
Semisweet chocolate chips	1 cup	250 mL
Chopped walnuts	½ cup	125 mL

Cream butter with brown sugar in medium bowl. Add granulated sugar and cream again. Add egg and vanilla and beat well.

Measure in flour, baking soda and salt. Stir until well blended.

Add chocolate chips and walnuts, stirring to combine. Scrape into greased 9 x 9 inch (22 x 22 cm) pan. Bake in 350°F (175°C) oven for 25 to 30 minutes until set and a nice brown color. Cool. Cuts into 36 squares.

Pictured on page 107.

The horse is such a respected, noble animal. So if you eat like one, why would you be any different?

MAGIC BARS

Nothing could be more simple and orderly.

Butter or hard margarine	½ cup	125 mL
Graham cracker crumbs	1½ cups	375 mL
Sweetened condensed milk	11 oz.	300 mL
Semisweet chocolate chips	1 cup	250 mL
Flake coconut	1⅓ cups	325 mL
Chopped walnuts	1 cup	250 mL

Melt butter in 9 x 13 inch (22 x 33 cm) pan. Sprinkle graham crumbs over butter in pan. Carefully spread condensed milk over top trying to get it as even as possible. Sprinkle chocolate chips over top, followed by coconut, then walnuts. With your hand, press down slightly all over. Bake in 350°F (175°C) oven for 25 to 30 minutes or until lightly browned. Cut when cool. Cuts into 54 squares. Since this is a very thin bar, it could be cut into 40 large squares.

Pictured on page 107.

Variation: An equal amount of butterscotch chips can be added along with the chocolate for an extra special taste treat.

1. Lemon Crumb Squares page 120
2. Cranberry Squares page 113
3. Quick Hurry Bars page 79
4. Marble Squares page 68
5. Easy Graham Bars page 104
6. Lemon Smacks page 138
7. Nutted Gumdrops page 112
8. Festive Fruit Cake page 67
9. Marzipan Bars page 73
10. Cranberry Oat Squares page 56
11. Chewy Candy Bars page 115
12. Nutty Spice Slice page 58
13. Graham Cracker Chew page 87
14. Fruit Marmalade Squares page 55
15. Three Layer Slice page 111
16. Grant's Special page 119
17. Australian Honey Bars page 97
18. Butterscotch Brownies page 61
19. Frieda's Number 89 page 109
20. Orange Date Bars page 118
21. Nutty Bars page 52
22. Raisin Squares page 103

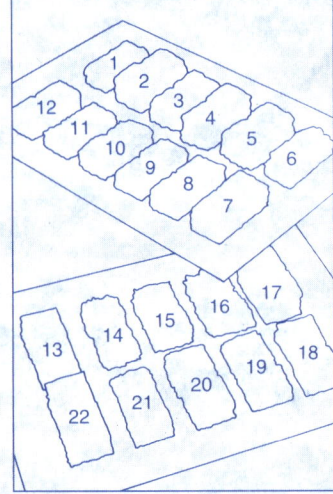

Lacquer Trays Courtesy Of:
Nazca

Lacquer Box Courtesy Of:
Ali Katu

Stained Glass Courtesy Of:
Winter Art Glass Studio Inc.

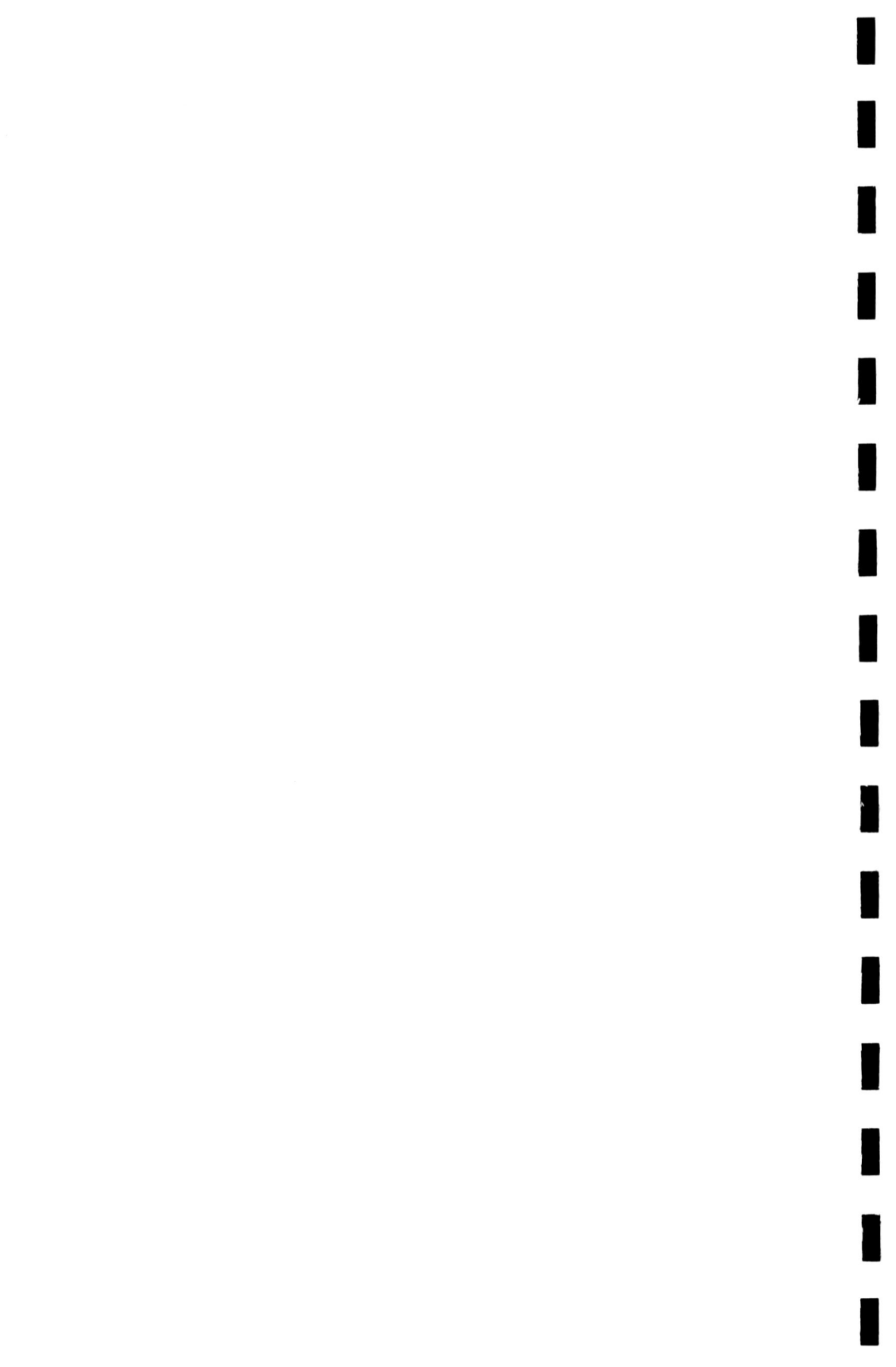

SWIRL SQUARES

No need to ice these. The swirl is made with the help of chocolate chips.

Butter or hard margarine, softened	½ cup	125 mL
Brown sugar, packed	½ cup	125 mL
Granulated sugar	¼ cup	60 mL
Vanilla	½ tsp.	2 mL
Large egg	1	1
All-purpose flour	1⅛ cups	280 mL
Baking soda	½ tsp.	2 mL
Salt	½ tsp.	2 mL
Chopped walnuts	½ cup	125 mL
Semisweet chocolate chips	1 cup	250 mL

In large bowl measure butter, both sugars, vanilla and egg. Beat together until blended.

Stir in flour, baking soda, salt and walnuts. Spread in greased 9 x 9 inch (22 x 22 cm) pan.

Sprinkle chocolate chips evenly over top. Bake in 375°F (190°C) oven for 1 to 2 minutes until chips are soft enough to marble. Run knife through batter to obtain a marble effect. Continue to bake for about 20 minutes more, until firm and a wooden pick inserted in center comes out clean. Cool. Cuts into 36 squares.

Pictured on page 89.

If you take your coffee without cream and sugar, any doughnuts you consume with it won't have a calorie in them.

CHOCOLATE PEPPERMINT SLICE

A nice surprise is the mint layer that you can barely see. It goes so well with the chocolate.

BOTTOM LAYER
All-purpose flour	1½ cups	350 mL
Brown sugar, packed	½ cup	125 mL
Butter or hard margarine, softened	¾ cup	175 mL
Medium coconut	1½ cups	350 mL

FILLING
Butter or hard margarine, softened	2 tbsp.	30 mL
Milk	2 tbsp.	30 mL
Icing (confectioner's) sugar	1½ cups	350 mL
Peppermint flavoring	½ tsp.	2 mL

TOP LAYER
Butter or hard margarine	6 tbsp.	100 mL
Chocolate drink powder	½ cup	125 mL

Bottom Layer: Crumble all 4 ingredients together. Press in ungreased 9 x 9 inch (22 x 22 cm) pan. Bake in 350°F (175°C) oven for 15 minutes. Cool completely.

Filling: Combine all 4 ingredients in bowl. Beat well. Spread over cooled bottom layer.

Top Layer: Melt butter in small saucepan over low heat. Add chocolate powder and stir. Remove from heat. Cool to room temperature and spoon in dabs over filling in pan. Spread smooth to cover. If it is too hot, it will melt the peppermint layer, making it impossible to cover. Allow to set. Cuts into 36 squares.

Pictured on page 143.

At your next coffee party anything consumed while your mind is busy with other things such as guests, coats, etc., cannot be absorbed.

NUT SMACKS

Butterscotch flavor, rich with nuts and brown sugar. An old family favorite.

BOTTOM LAYER		
Brown sugar, packed	½ cup	125 mL
Egg yolks (large)	2	2
Vanilla	1 tsp.	5 mL
Butter or hard margarine, softened	½ cup	125 mL
Salt	¼ tsp.	1 mL
All-purpose flour	1½ cups	375 mL
Baking powder	1 tsp.	5 mL
SECOND LAYER		
Egg whites (large), room temperature	2	2
Brown sugar, packed	1 cup	250 mL
Chopped walnuts	1 cup	250 mL

Bottom Layer: Crumble all 7 ingredients together well in large bowl. Press firmly in ungreased 9 x 9 inch (22 x 22 cm) pan. Set aside.

Second Layer: Beat egg whites until frothy. Add brown sugar ⅓ at a time, beating until stiff. Fold in walnuts. Spoon over unbaked base, spreading evenly. Bake in 350°F (175°C) oven for about 25 minutes until golden. Cool. Covering pan allows meringue to soften for easier cutting. Cuts into 36 squares.

Pictured on page 143.

Any food eaten during an intimate candlelight meal doesn't contain calories. It can't be starch, it's seduction.

LEMON GRAHAM SLICE

This one is for lemon lovers with its exceptionally lemony flavor.

BOTTOM LAYER		
Butter or hard margarine	½ cup	125 mL
Graham cracker crumbs	1½ cups	375 mL
Brown sugar, packed	⅓ cup	75 mL
Baking powder	½ tsp.	2 mL
Salt	⅛ tsp.	0.5 mL
SECOND LAYER		
Sweetened condensed milk	11 oz.	300 mL
Lemon juice, fresh or bottled	½ cup	125 mL
Vanilla	1 tsp.	5 mL

Bottom Layer: Melt butter in medium saucepan. Stir in graham crumbs, sugar, baking powder and salt. Pack in ungreased 9 × 9 inch (22 × 22 cm) pan. Set aside.

Second Layer: Combine condensed milk, lemon juice and vanilla in bowl. Spread over bottom layer. Bake in 350°F (175°C) oven for 20 to 25 minutes. Cool. Cuts into 36 squares.

Pictured on page 89.

CHOCOLATE COCONUT MELTS

And it does melt in your mouth.

Sweetened condensed milk	11 oz.	300 mL
Unsweetened chocolate baking squares, cut up	2 × 1 oz.	2 × 28 g
Salt	¼ tsp.	1 mL
Flake coconut	2⅔ cups	600 mL
Vanilla	1 tsp.	5 mL

Combine condensed milk, chocolate and salt in heavy pot or top of double boiler over hot water. Stir every once in awhile as the chocolate melts. Remove from heat when melted and thickened.

Add coconut and vanilla. Stir to blend. Scrape into greased 8 × 8 inch (20 × 20 cm) pan. Bake in 350°F (175°C) oven for 20 minutes until set. Cool. Cuts into 25 squares.

Pictured on page 107.

CARAMEL SHORTBREAD

An upside down toffee-like confection.

BOTTOM LAYER		
All-purpose flour	1 cup	250 mL
Icing (confectioner's) sugar	½ cup	125 mL
Butter or hard margarine, softened	½ cup	125 mL
SECOND LAYER		
Butter or hard margarine	½ cup	125 mL
Dark corn syrup	¼ cup	60 mL
Brown sugar, packed	½ cup	125 mL
Unflavored gelatin	1 tsp.	5 mL
Sweetened condensed milk	⅔ cup	150 mL

Bottom Layer: Measure all 3 ingredients into bowl. Crumble together well. Press in ungreased 8 x 8 inch (20 x 20 cm) pan. Bake in 350°F (175°C) oven for 15 to 20 minutes. Cool.

Second Layer: Melt butter and corn syrup in heavy saucepan.

Measure brown sugar in cup. Stir in gelatin to mix thoroughly. Add to saucepan stirring to dissolve.

Add condensed milk. Stir, bringing to a boil. Boil 5 minutes, stirring constantly. It burns very easily when boiling. Remove from heat. Beat with spoon for 7 to 10 minutes until it is thick and shiny, like toffee. You may need to take a moment's rest now and then as you beat. Pour over first layer. Chill overnight. Invert on plastic wrap. This makes it much easier to cut through. Cuts into 25 squares.

Pictured on page 107.

Play it safe. Take your "just desserts" now. That way you get to have a choice!

CINNAMON BARS

Make a spicy bar for a change.

BOTTOM LAYER		
All-purpose flour	1½ cups	375 mL
Granulated sugar	⅓ cup	75 mL
Ground cinnamon	1½ tsp.	7 mL
Baking powder	½ tsp.	2 mL
Salt	⅛ tsp.	0.5 mL
Butter or hard margarine, softened	½ cup	125 mL
Egg yolk (large)	1	1
SECOND LAYER		
Egg white (large)	1	1
Granulated sugar	½ cup	125 mL
Chopped walnuts	½ cup	125 mL
ICING		
Butter or hard margarine	¼ cup	60 mL
Brown sugar, packed	½ cup	125 mL
Milk	2 tbsp.	30 mL
Icing (confectioner's) sugar	1 cup	250 mL

Bottom Layer: Measure all 7 ingredients into bowl. Crumble together well. Press in ungreased 8 x 8 inch (20 x 20 cm) pan. Set aside.

Second Layer: Beat egg white until frothy. Add sugar gradually while continuing to beat until stiff. Fold in walnuts. Spread over first layer. Bake in 350°F (175°C) oven for about 25 minutes until golden. Cool.

Icing: Put butter, brown sugar and milk in saucepan. Bring to a boil over medium heat. Simmer gently 2 minutes. Remove from heat. Cool to lukewarm.

Stir in icing sugar, adding more if too soft or adding more milk, if too stiff to spread. Smooth over bars. Let set. Cuts into 25 squares.

Pictured on page 107.

BIKINI BARS

Almost everybody's choice when given their pick of the lot.

Sweetened condensed milk	⅔ cup	150 mL
Medium coconut	2½ cups	575 mL
Vanilla	1 tsp.	5 mL
Salt	⅛ tsp.	0.5 mL
Chopped walnuts	½ cup	125 mL
Chopped dates	2 cups	450 mL
Chopped maraschino cherries, well-drained	¼ cup	60 mL
ICING		
Icing (confectioner's) sugar	1½ cups	375 mL
Butter or hard margarine, softened	3 tbsp.	50 mL
Vanilla	½ tsp.	2 mL
Water or milk	1½ tbsp.	25 mL
DRIZZLE		
Unsweetened chocolate baking square, cut up	1 × 1 oz.	1 × 28 g

Measure first 7 ingredients into large bowl in order given. Stir to combine. Press in greased 9 × 9 inch (22 × 22 cm) pan. Bake in 350°F (175°C) oven for 30 minutes. Cool.

Icing: Beat all 4 ingredients in small bowl, adjusting liquid or icing sugar as needed for proper spreading consistency. Spread over cooled bars.

Drizzle: Melt chocolate in small saucepan over low heat or set in pan of hot water. Stir to hasten melting. Drizzle from end of teaspoon over iced bars. Let set. Cuts into 36 squares.

Pictured on page 89.

BUTTERSCOTCH TOFFEE BARS

Melted candy bar is the secret to the toffee layer.

BOTTOM LAYER

All-purpose flour	1 cup	250 mL
Brown sugar, packed	6 tbsp.	100 mL
Salt	⅛ tsp.	0.5 mL
Butter or hard margarine, softened	½ cup	125 mL

SECOND LAYER

Bar of butterscotch toffee (such as McIntosh), broken up	6 oz.	170 g
Corn syrup, light or dark	1 tbsp.	15 mL
Water	1 tbsp.	15 mL
Butter or hard margarine	2 tbsp.	30 mL
Salt	⅛ tsp.	0.5 mL
Chopped walnuts	⅔ cup	150 mL

Bottom Layer: Measure all 4 ingredients in medium bowl. Crumble together well. Press in ungreased 9 x 9 inch (22 x 22 cm) pan. Bake in 375°F (190°C) oven for 10 to 12 minutes.

Second Layer: Combine first 5 ingredients in saucepan. Melt over low heat, stirring often.

Add walnuts. Stir. Pour over bottom layer. Bake in 375°F (190°C) oven for 8 to 10 minutes. Cool. Cuts into 25 squares.

Pictured on page 107.

While waiting and waiting for a friend to meet you on a certain corner and you buy snacks from a corner stand, that won't count on your diet. Actually you are using the food as a legal device to avoid a loitering charge.

CARAMEL TOFFEE SQUARES

Now these are a real treat. Make this one of the first recipes to try.

BOTTOM LAYER		
All-purpose flour	1¼ cups	300 mL
Granulated sugar	¼ cup	60 mL
Butter or hard margarine, softened	½ cup	125 mL
More butter or hard margarine, softened	2 tsp.	10 mL
SECOND LAYER		
Butter or hard margarine	½ cup	125 mL
Brown sugar, packed	½ cup	125 ml
Corn syrup, light or dark	2 tbsp.	30 mL
Sweetened condensed milk	½ cup	125 mL
TOP LAYER		
Semisweet chocolate chips	2 cups	500 mL

Bottom Layer: Crumble all 4 ingredients well. Pack in ungreased 9 x 9 inch (22 x 22 cm) pan. Bake in 350°F (175°C) oven for 20 minutes.

Second Layer: Combine all 4 ingredients in heavy saucepan. Bring to boil over medium heat. Boil 5 minutes, stirring constantly, as it will burn easily. Remove from heat. Beat with spoon slowly until it shows signs of thickening. Pour over bottom layer.

Top Layer: Melt chocolate chips in saucepan over low heat or over hot water, stirring often. Spread over second layer. Chill. Cuts into 36 squares.

Pictured on page 107.

If you are really on a strict diet, eat all the maple syrup you can. Since it is a wood product you wouldn't count it any more than you would count toothpicks.

BROWNIES

Not only is this the easiest and fastest brownie to make, it is also the best tasting ever.

Butter or hard margarine	½ cup	125 mL
Cocoa	¼ cup	60 mL
Large eggs	2	2
Granulated sugar	1 cup	250 mL
All-purpose flour	¾ cup	175 mL
Chopped walnuts	½ cup	125 mL
Salt	⅛ tsp.	0.5 mL
ICING		
Icing (confectioner's) sugar	1⅓ cups	325 mL
Cocoa	⅓ cup	75 mL
Butter or hard margarine, softened	3 tbsp.	50 mL
Hot prepared coffee or water	1½ tbsp.	25 mL

In small saucepan melt butter and cocoa, stirring as it melts. Remove from heat.

Beat eggs in medium bowl until frothy. Add sugar, flour, walnuts and salt. Don't stir yet. Pour cocoa mixture over top and stir all together. Scrape batter into greased 8 x 8 inch (20 x 20 cm) pan. Bake in 350°F (175°C) oven for 25 to 30 minutes until the edges begin to show signs of pulling away from the sides of the pan. A wooden pick inserted in the center should come out moist with no batter clinging to it.

Icing: Beat all 4 ingredients together, adding more liquid if mixture is too firm to spread easily and more icing sugar if too soft. Spread over warm brownies. Allow to set before cutting. Cuts into 25 squares.

Pictured on page 107.

SESAME SQUARES

These squares have a chewy texture and a nutty taste.

BOTTOM LAYER		
Butter or hard margarine, softened	½ cup	125 mL
Brown sugar, packed	½ cup	125 mL
All-purpose flour	1½ cups	375 mL
Large egg	1	1
FILLING		
Raspberry or apricot jam	1 cup	250 mL
TOP LAYER		
Large eggs	2	2
Brown sugar, packed	1 cup	250 mL
Sesame seeds, toasted in moderate oven until golden	½ cup	125 mL
All-purpose flour	1 tbsp.	15 mL

Bottom Layer: Mix and crumble all 4 ingredients in bowl until mealy. Press in ungreased 9 x 9 inch (22 x 22 cm) pan. Bake in 350°F (175°C) oven for 10 minutes. Cool for 10 minutes.

Filling: Spoon small dabs of jam here and there over bottom layer. Spread.

Top Layer: Beat eggs with brown sugar. Stir in sesame seeds and flour. Spread over jam. Bake in 350°F (175°C) oven for about 25 minutes or until set and a nice golden color. Cool. Cuts into 36 squares.

Pictured on page 107.

Paré Pointer

While visiting a friend in the hospital and you are sampling his chocolates, you are not to worry. Just read the card and you will see it states very clearly that it is all intended for him.

LEMON SMACKS

Such a light and lemony square — food for the fairies. Best eaten the same day it's made. Do not freeze.

BOTTOM LAYER
All-purpose flour	1½ cups	375 mL
Brown sugar, packed	½ cup	125 mL
Butter or hard margarine, softened	½ cup	125 mL
Egg yolks (large)	2	2
Baking powder	1 tsp.	5 mL
Salt	¼ tsp.	1 mL

FILLING
Granulated sugar	½ cup	125 mL
Cornstarch	¼ cup	60 mL
Large egg, beaten	1	1
Water	1 cup	250 mL
Lemon juice (fresh is best)	¼ cup	60 mL
Salt	⅛ tsp.	0.5 mL

TOP LAYER
Egg whites (large), room temperature	2	2
Brown sugar, packed	1 cup	250 mL
Chopped walnuts (optional, but good)	½ cup	125 mL

Bottom Layer: Measure all 6 ingredients into bowl. Mix and crumble together until mealy in texture. Press in ungreased 9 × 9 inch (22 × 22 cm) pan. Set aside.

Filling: Mix sugar and cornstarch in small saucepan. Stir in egg. Add water, lemon juice and salt. Heat and stir until it boils and thickens. Spoon dabs here and there over bottom layer. Spread evenly.

Top Layer: Beat egg whites until frothy. Add brown sugar ⅓ at a time, beating until stiff. Fold in walnuts if using. Spread over lemon layer. Bake in 350°F (175°C) oven for about 25 minutes until light golden brown. Cool. Cut with hot knife dipped in hot water between each cut. Cuts into 36 squares.

Pictured on page 125.

While at a church potluck supper, eat lots. Food for the soul has no calories.

LEMON MARDI GRAS

This is a one-layer square. Although it does take two beating times and one folding-in time, you can still have it in the oven right smartly. Sort of cakey.

Egg whites (large)	2	2
Granulated sugar	½ cup	125 mL
Butter or hard margarine, softened	¼ cup	60 mL
Granulated sugar	½ cup	125 mL
Egg yolks (large)	2	2
Lemon juice, fresh or bottled	3 tbsp.	50 mL
Grated lemon rind	1 tsp.	5 mL
All-purpose flour	¾ cup	175 mL
Baking powder	½ tsp.	2 mL
Salt	¼ tsp.	1 mL
Chopped walnuts	⅓ cup	75 mL
GLAZE		
Granulated sugar	¼ cup	60 mL
Lemon juice, fresh or bottled	3 tbsp.	50 mL

Beat egg whites until foamy. Add first amount of sugar gradually while beating until stiff. Set aside.

Mix butter, second amount of sugar, egg yolks, lemon juice and rind together. Beat well.

Stir in flour, baking powder, salt and walnuts. Fold in beaten egg whites. Scrape into greased 8 × 8 inch (20 × 20 cm) pan. Bake in 400°F (205°C) oven for 20 to 25 minutes.

Glaze: Put sugar and lemon juice into saucepan. Heat and stir to dissolve sugar. Spoon slowly over hot squares. Cool. Cuts into 25 squares.

Pictured on page 107.

BUTTER TART BARS

These have a rich caramel taste with a gooey, chewy texture.

BOTTOM LAYER		
Butter or hard margarine, softened	½ cup	125 mL
Brown sugar, packed	⅓ cup	75 mL
All-purpose flour	1¼ cups	300 mL
SECOND LAYER		
Large eggs	2	2
Brown sugar, packed	1 cup	250 mL
All-purpose flour	1 tsp.	5 mL
Baking powder	½ tsp.	2 mL
Salt	¼ tsp.	1 mL
Butter or hard margarine, melted	¼ cup	60 mL
Vanilla	1 tsp.	5 mL
Raisins	1½ cups	375 mL
Chopped walnuts	½ cup	125 mL

Bottom Layer: Crumble all 3 ingredients together in bowl. Press in ungreased 9 x 9 inch (22 x 22 cm) pan. Bake in 350°F (175°C) oven for 15 minutes.

Second Layer: Mix eggs and brown sugar with spoon. Add the rest of ingredients. Stir. Spread over bottom layer. Bake in 350°F (175°C) oven for about 20 minutes or until light brown. Cool. Cuts into 36 squares.

Pictured on cover.

Take huge helpings. Don't let it be said you eat like a bird. Ever seen a vulture?

APRICOT CHEWS

The dried apricots give this a lot of flavor. The finer the apricots are cut up, the better.

BOTTOM LAYER
Butter or hard margarine, softened	½ cup	125 mL
All-purpose flour	1¼ cups	300 mL
Brown sugar, packed	½ cup	125 mL

SECOND LAYER
Large eggs	2	2
All-purpose flour	⅓ cup	75 mL
Baking powder	1 tsp.	5 mL
Sweetened condensed milk	11 oz.	300 mL
Flake coconut	1⅓ cups	325 mL
Finely chopped dried apricots	1 cup	250 mL

Bottom Layer: Mix all 3 ingredients together. Crumble until mealy. Press in ungreased 9 x 9 inch (22 x 22 cm) pan. Bake in 350°F (175°C) oven for 10 minutes.

Second Layer: Beat eggs in bowl until frothy. Measure in rest of ingredients. Stir well to mix. Spread over first layer. Bake in 350°F (175°C) oven for 25 to 30 minutes or until firm to touch. Cool. Store well-covered. Cuts into 36 squares.

Pictured on page 89.

Ever been in a grocery store and been handed samples of food to eat? Make the rounds twice to be sure you get your share. That is advertising, not calories.

RASPBERRY MERINGUE

A pretty treat to enhance any plate of goodies.

BOTTOM LAYER		
All-purpose flour	1½ cups	375 mL
Brown sugar, packed	¾ cup	175 mL
Baking powder	2 tsp.	10 mL
Butter or hard margarine, softened	½ cup	125 mL
Egg yolks (large)	2	2
FILLING		
Raspberry jam or other red jam	1 cup	250 mL
TOP LAYER		
Egg whites (large), room temperature	2	2
Brown sugar, packed	¾ cup	175 mL
Medium coconut	1 cup	250 mL

Bottom Layer: Crumble all 5 ingredients together. Press in ungreased 9 x 9 inch (22 x 22 cm) pan. Set aside.

Filling: Stir jam vigorously. Begin by dropping small blobs of jam here and there over bottom layer, then spread carefully.

Top Layer: Beat egg whites until frothy. Add brown sugar ⅓ at a time, beating until stiff. Fold in coconut. Spread over jam layer. Bake in 350°F (175°C) oven for 25 to 30 minutes. Cool. Cut with sharp knife, dipped in hot water between cuts. Cuts into 36 squares.

Pictured on page 35.

1. Double Brownies page 74
2. Apricot Zings page 86
3. Matrimonial Squares page 50
4. Orange Squares page 105
5. Apple Squares page 70
6. Scotch Shortbread page 56
7. Chocolate Nut Shortcake page 57
8. Chewy Nut Bars page 110
9. Walnut Bars page 145
10. Almond Date Squares page 91
11. Chocolate Peppermint Slice page 128.
12. Cheese Apple Squares page 76
13. Caribbean Bars page 63
14. Nut Smacks page 129
15. Lemon Squares page 116

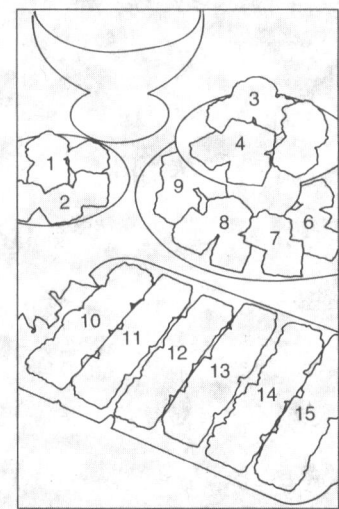

Glassware Courtesy Of:
Eaton's China Dept.

Tablecloth Courtesy Of:
Pacific Linen

WALNUT BARS

It's a safe bet that everyone will like this better-known bar.

BOTTOM LAYER		
All-purpose flour	1¼ cups	300 mL
Butter or hard margarine, softened	½ cup	125 mL
Brown sugar, packed (see Note)	⅓ cup	75 mL
SECOND LAYER		
Large eggs	2	2
Vanilla	1 tsp.	5 mL
Brown sugar, packed	1¼ cups	300 mL
All-purpose flour	1 tsp.	5 mL
Baking powder	½ tsp.	2 mL
Salt	¼ tsp.	1 mL
Chopped walnuts	1 cup	250 mL
Medium coconut	½ cup	125 mL
ICING		
Icing (confectioner's) sugar	1½ cups	375 mL
Butter or hard margarine, softened	3 tbsp.	50 mL
Vanilla	½ tsp.	2 mL
Water or milk	1½ tbsp.	25 mL

Bottom Layer: Crumble all 3 ingredients together well. Press in ungreased 9 x 9 inch (22 x 22 cm) pan. Bake in 350°F (175°C) oven for 10 minutes.

Second Layer: Beat eggs slightly. Add next 7 ingredients in order given. Stir well and pour over bottom layer. Bake in 350°F (175°C) oven for about 25 minutes until a rich brown color. Cool.

Icing: Beat all 4 ingredients in bowl, adding more icing sugar or water if needed for easy spreading. Smooth over cooled bars.

Note: Use ¼ cup (60 mL) granulated sugar instead of brown sugar in bottom layer for a whiter base.

Pictured on page 143.

Variation: Sprinkle ⅓ cup (75 mL) crushed walnuts over icing.

PEANUT BUTTER CHIP SQUARES

More like a confection. It's so good.

BOTTOM LAYER
Butter or hard margarine	½ cup	125 mL
Graham cracker crumbs	1¼ cups	300 mL
Brown sugar, packed	½ cup	125 mL
All-purpose flour	⅓ cup	75 mL

SECOND LAYER
Sweetened condensed milk	11 oz.	300 mL
Medium coconut	2 cups	500 mL

TOP LAYER
Semisweet chocolate chips	2 cups	500 mL
Smooth peanut butter	2 tbsp.	30 mL

Bottom Layer: Melt butter in medium saucepan. Stir in graham crumbs, sugar and flour. Press in ungreased 9 x 9 inch (22 x 22 cm) pan. Bake in 350°F (175°C) oven for 10 minutes.

Second Layer: Stir condensed milk with coconut. Do this just before spreading so coconut doesn't have time to soak up milk which makes it more difficult to spread. Spread over first layer. Return to oven and bake for 10 minutes or until it shows signs of browning lightly.

Top Layer: Melt chocolate chips and peanut butter in heavy saucepan over low heat, stirring often. Spread over second layer. Cool. Cuts into 36 squares.

Pictured on page 89.

CHOCOLATE SMACKS

For a melt-in-your-mouth snack, try this!

BOTTOM LAYER
All-purpose flour	1¼ cups	300 mL
Cocoa	¼ cup	60 mL
Brown sugar, packed	½ cup	125 mL
Butter or hard margarine, softened	½ cup	125 mL
Egg yolks (large)	2	2
Baking powder	1 tsp.	5 mL
Salt	¼ tsp.	1 mL

SECOND LAYER
Egg whites (large), room temperature	2	2
Brown sugar, packed	1 cup	250 mL
Cocoa	2 tbsp.	30 mL
Chopped walnuts	1 cup	250 mL

Bottom Layer: Measure all 7 ingredients into bowl. Crumble together. Press in ungreased 9 x 9 inch (22 x 22 cm) pan. Set aside.

Second Layer: Beat egg whites until frothy. Add brown sugar ⅓ at a time and beat after each addition until stiff. Add cocoa and beat to blend.

Fold in walnuts. Spread over bottom layer. Bake in 350°F (175°C) oven for about 25 minutes until golden brown. Cut with sharp knife, dipped in hot water between cuts. Cuts into 36 squares.

Pictured on page 107.

MYSTERY CAKE

It is a mystery to someone who doesn't cook as to just what makes this so delicious. It is thick and high.

BOTTOM LAYER		
Butter or hard margarine, softened	1 cup	250 mL
All-purpose flour	2 cups	500 mL
Granulated or brown sugar, packed	½ cup	125 mL
SECOND LAYER		
Large eggs	2	2
Brown sugar, packed	½ cup	125 mL
All-purpose flour	2 tbsp.	30 mL
Baking powder	½ tsp.	2 mL
Chopped dates	1 cup	250 mL
Chopped walnuts	1 cup	250 mL
Medium coconut	1½ cups	350 mL
ICING		
Icing (confectioner's) sugar	1½ cups	375 mL
Butter or hard margarine, softened	3 tbsp.	50 mL
Vanilla	½ tsp.	2 mL
Water or milk	1½ tbsp.	25 mL

Bottom Layer: Crumble all 3 ingredients together in bowl until mealy. Press in ungreased 9 x 9 inch (22 x 22 cm) pan. Set aside.

Second Layer: Beat eggs slightly in bowl. Add rest of ingredients. Stir until combined. Spread over bottom layer. Bake in 350°F (175°C) oven for 30 minutes until brown. Cool.

Icing: Beat all 4 ingredients together, adjusting liquid and icing sugar to make proper spreading consistency. Spread over cooled bars. Cuts into 36 squares.

Pictured on page 107.

RAISIN SPICE BARS

Unlike Raisin Squares, these have spices in them which make them seem like a different type of bar altogether.

Brown sugar, packed	½ cup	125 mL
Water	½ cup	125 mL
Butter or hard margarine	¼ cup	60 mL
Raisins	1 cup	250 mL
Ground cinnamon	1 tsp.	5 mL
Ground nutmeg	¼ tsp.	1 mL
Ground cloves	¼ tsp.	1 mL
Salt	½ tsp.	2 mL
Baking soda	½ tsp.	2 mL
Water	2 tsp.	10 mL
All-purpose flour	1 cup	250 mL
Baking powder	1 tsp.	5 mL
ICING		
Icing (confectioner's) sugar	1½ cups	375 mL
Butter or hard margarine, softened	3 tbsp.	50 mL
Lemon juice, fresh or bottled	1½ tbsp.	25 mL

In large saucepan combine first 8 ingredients. Bring to boil over medium heat. Simmer 3 minutes. Remove from heat.

Mix baking soda with second amount of water and add to hot mixture. Stir. Cool.

Measure flour and baking powder into cooled mixture. Stir to mix. Scrape into greased 8 x 8 inch (20 x 20 cm) pan. Bake in 350°F (175°C) oven for about 25 to 30 minutes until set.

Icing: Beat icing sugar and butter together in bowl. Mix in some lemon juice and taste. If too lemony, add water instead of more lemon juice. To get a lemon color, add a wee bit of yellow food coloring. Spread over cooled bars. Cuts into 25 squares.

Pictured on page 107.

Variation: Use the icing for Caramel Slice, page 65.

POPPY SEED SQUARES

Time to try a different flavor. The caramel icing seems to complement this square but it is very good without any icing.

Poppy seeds	½ cup	125 mL
Milk	2 tbsp.	30 mL
All-purpose flour	1¾ cups	400 mL
Granulated sugar	1¼ cups	300 mL
Baking powder	1 tsp.	5 mL
Baking soda	¼ tsp.	1 mL
Salt	½ tsp.	2 mL
Butter or hard margarine, melted	½ cup	125 mL
Honey	⅓ cup	75 mL
Large eggs	2	2
Vanilla	1 tsp.	5 mL
Medium coconut	1 cup	225 mL
ICING		
Brown sugar, packed	¾ cup	175 mL
Butter or hard margarine	¼ cup	60 mL
Milk	2 tbsp.	30 mL
Icing (confectioner's) sugar	1½ cups	375 mL

Measure poppy seeds in cup. Cover with milk and let stand.

Measure flour, sugar, baking powder, baking soda and salt into bowl. Stir. Add butter, honey, eggs and vanilla. Beat until blended.

Stir in coconut and poppy seed mixture. Spread in greased 9 x 13 inch (22 x 33 cm) pan. Bake in 350°F (175°C) oven for 25 to 30 minutes. Cool.

Icing: Bring brown sugar, butter and milk to a boil in saucepan over medium heat. Stir to dissolve sugar for a minute or so. Remove from heat. Cool.

Add icing sugar. Add more icing sugar or milk for proper spreading consistency. Spread over cooled bars. Cuts into 54 squares.

Pictured on page 89.

ALMOND BARS

Almonds seem to be a festive treat. These bars are slightly spicy.

BOTTOM LAYER
Butter or hard margarine, softened	⅔ cup	150 mL
Granulated sugar	6 tbsp.	100 mL
All-purpose flour	1½ cups	375 mL

SECOND LAYER
Whipping cream	½ cup	125 mL
Ground almonds	½ cup	125 mL
Brown sugar	1 tbsp.	15 mL
Ground cinnamon	1 tsp.	5 mL
Egg yolk (large), fork beaten	1	1

GLAZE
Icing (confectioner's) sugar	½ cup	125 mL
Lemon juice, fresh or bottled	1 tbsp.	15 mL

Bottom Layer: Crumble all 3 ingredients together in bowl. Pack in ungreased 8 x 8 inch (20 x 20 cm) pan. Bake in 325°F (160°C) oven for 10 minutes. Cool.

Second Layer: Whip cream until stiff. Fold in almonds, brown sugar, cinnamon and egg yolk. Spread over cooled bottom layer. Bake in 325°F (160°C) oven for about 40 minutes. Cool.

Glaze: Stir icing sugar and lemon juice together in small bowl, adding more icing sugar or juice as needed so it will just barely pour from spoon. Spread over bars. Allow to set. Cuts into 25 squares.

Pictured on page 107.

MEASUREMENT TABLES

Throughout this book measurements are given in Conventional and Metric measure. To compensate for differences between the two measurements due to rounding, a full metric measure is not always used. The cup used is the standard 8 fluid ounce. Temperature is given in degrees Fahrenheit and Celsius. Baking pan measurements are in inches and centimetres as well as quarts and litres. An exact metric conversion is given below as well as the working equivalent (Standard Measure).

OVEN TEMPERATURES

Fahrenheit (°F)	Celsius (°C)
175°	80°
200°	95°
225°	110°
250°	120°
275°	140°
300°	150°
325°	160°
350°	175°
375°	190°
400°	205°
425°	220°
450°	230°
475°	240°
500°	260°

SPOONS

Conventional Measure	Metric Exact Conversion Millilitre (mL)	Metric Standard Measure Millilitre (mL)
1/8 teaspoon (tsp.)	0.6 mL	0.5 mL
1/4 teaspoon (tsp.)	1.2 mL	1 mL
1/2 teaspoon (tsp.)	2.4 mL	2 mL
1 teaspoon (tsp.)	4.7 mL	5 mL
2 teaspoons (tsp.)	9.4 mL	10 mL
1 tablespoon (tbsp.)	14.2 mL	15 mL

CUPS

Conventional Measure	Metric Exact Conversion	Metric Standard Measure
1/4 cup (4 tbsp.)	56.8 mL	50 mL
1/3 cup (5 1/3 tbsp.)	75.6 mL	75 mL
1/2 cup (8 tbsp.)	113.7 mL	125 mL
2/3 cup (10 2/3 tbsp.)	151.2 mL	150 mL
3/4 cup (12 tbsp.)	170.5 mL	175 mL
1 cup (16 tbsp.)	227.3 mL	250 mL
4 1/2 cups	1022.9 mL	1000 mL (1 L)

PANS

Conventional Inches	Metric Centimetres
8x8 inch	20x20 cm
9x9 inch	22x22 cm
9x13 inch	22x33 cm
10x15 inch	25x38 cm
11x17 inch	28x43 cm
8x2 inch round	20x5 cm
9x2 inch round	22x5 cm
10x4 1/2 inch tube	25x11 cm
8x4x3 inch loaf	20x10x7 cm
9x5x3 inch loaf	22x12x7 cm

DRY MEASUREMENTS

Conventional Measure Ounces (oz.)	Metric Exact Conversion Grams (g)	Metric Standard Measure Grams (g)
1 oz.	28.3 g	30 g
2 oz.	56.7 g	55 g
3 oz.	85.0 g	85 g
4 oz.	113.4 g	125 g
5 oz.	141.7 g	140 g
6 oz.	170.1 g	170 g
7 oz.	198.4 g	200 g
8 oz.	226.8 g	250 g
16 oz.	453.6 g	500 g
32 oz.	907.2 g	1000 g (1 kg)

CASSEROLES (Canada & Britain)

Standard Size Casserole	Exact Metric Measure
1 qt. (5 cups)	1.13 L
1 1/2 qts. (7 1/2 cups)	1.69 L
2 qts. (10 cups)	2.25 L
2 1/2 qts. (12 1/2 cups)	2.81 L
3 qts. (15 cups)	3.38 L
4 qts. (20 cups)	4.5 L
5 qts. (25 cups)	5.63 L

CASSEROLES (United States)

Standard Size Casserole	Exact Metric Measure
1 qt. (4 cups)	900 mL
1 1/2 qts. (6 cups)	1.35 L
2 qts. (8 cups)	1.8 L
2 1/2 qts. (10 cups)	2.25 L
3 qts. (12 cups)	2.7 L
4 qts. (16 cups)	3.6 L
5 qts. (20 cups)	4.5 L

INDEX

Almond Bars 151
Almond Date Squares 91
Apple
   Cheese Apple Squares 76
   Frieda's Number 89 109
Apple Squares 70
Apricot Chews 141
Apricot Roll 19
Apricot Zings 86
Australian Honey Bars 97

Baba Rum Roll 12
Baked Fruit Roll 103
Banana
   Cherry Wonder 30
Banana Bars 66
Banana Oat Squares 49
Bikini Bars 133
Black Bottom Slice 51
Bridge Peel Dainties 24
Brownies 136
Brownies
   Butterscotch Brownies 61
   Cream Cheese Brownies 80
   Double Brownies 74
   Marble Squares 68
   Pineapple Brownies 69
   Saucepan Brownies 23
Butterscotch Brownies 61
Butterscotch Coconut Squares 27
Butterscotch Confetti 33
Butterscotch Toffee Bars 134
Butter Tart Bars 140

Caramel Shortbread 131
Caramel Slice 65
Caramel Toffee Squares 135
Caribbean Bars 63
Cereal
   Chocolate Crisps 10
   Chocolate Peanut Squares 32
   Fudgy Macaroons 20
   Krispy Krunch Bars 38
   Peanut Butter Rice Krispies 9
   Peanut Krispie Squares 41
   Puffed Wheat Squares 26
   Rice Krispies 9
Cereal Slice 15
Cheese Apple Squares 76

Cherries
   Bikini Bars 133
   Caribbean Bars 63
   Chocolate Carousels 31
   Chocolate Cherry Creams 33
   Chocolate Cherry Slice 64
   Chocolate Fruit Squares 99
   Chocolate Roll 8
   Cream Cheese Brownies 80
   Fancy Whip Up 11
   Festive Fruit 43
   Fruit Marmalade Squares 55
   Fruit Roll 20
   Fruity Fruit Slice 62
   Oh Henry Bars 44
   Snow Log 24
Cherry Almond Squares 79
Cherry Squares 92
Cherry Triangles 77
Cherry Wonder 30
Chewy Candy Bars 115
Chewy Nut Bars 110
Chinese Chews 121
Chip Crumbles 82
Chocolate
   Baba Rum Roll 12
   Black Bottom Slice 51
   Brownies 136
   Caramel Toffee Squares 135
   Chewy Nut Bars 110
   Chip Crumbles 82
   Chow Mein Noodles 34
   Cream Cheese Brownies 80
   Double Brownies 74
   Easy Graham Bars 104
   Five-Cup Slice 78
   Flat Truffles 16
   Grant's Special 119
   Magic Bars 124
   Marble Squares 68
   Marshmallow Roll 38
   Midnight Mints 13
   Millionaire Squares 45
   Nanaimo Bars 40
   Peanut Butter Bars 82
   Peanut Butter Chip Squares 146
   Peanut Krispie Squares 41
   Pineapple Brownies 69

Puffed Wheat Squares 26
Saucepan Brownies 23
S'Mores 10
Swirl Squares 127
Tweed Squares 100
Chocolate Boil 21
Chocolate Carousels 31
Chocolate Cherry Creams 33
Chocolate Cherry Slice 64
Chocolate Chip Squares 123
Chocolate Coconut Layer 25
Chocolate Coconut Melts 130
Chocolate Confetti 28
Chocolate Crisps 10
Chocolate Date Nut Squares............ 88
Chocolate Fruit Squares................... 99
Chocolate Nut Shortcake 57
Chocolate Oh Henry Squares 42
Chocolate Orange Drops.................. 96
Chocolate Peanut Squares 32
Chocolate Peppermint Slice 128
Chocolate Roll 8
Chocolate Smacks 147
Chocolate TV Roll 28
Chocolate Walnut Slice 84
Chow Mein Noodles 34
Cinnamon Bars 132
Coconut Graham Cake..................... 84
Coconut Lemon Bars.......................101
Coconut Roll 12
Coffee
Tropical Treat 29
Condensed Milk
Apricot Chews 141
Bikini Bars 133
Bridge Peel Dainties 24
Caramel Shortbread....................131
Caramel Toffee Squares 134
Chewy Candy Bars 115
Chocolate Coconut Melts 130
Condensed Squares 101
Five-Cup Slice............................... 78
Graham Mint Roll 19
Lemon Graham Slice 130
Magic Bars 124
Marshmallow Roll........................... 38
Neapolitan Squares 83
Peanut Butter Chip Squares 146

Peanut Butter Rice Krispies 9
Quick Hurry Bars............................. 79
Rainbow Pastel 25
Condensed Squares..................................101
Cranberry
Frieda's Number 89 109
Cranberry Oat Squares 56
Cranberry Squares 113
Cream Cheese
Chewy Candy Bars 115
Chocolate Orange Drops 96
Pineapple Log 39
Snow Log 24
Cream Cheese Brownies 80
Date
Almond Date Squares 91
Apricot Roll....................................... 19
Baked Fruit Roll 103
Bikini Bars 133
Bridge Peel Dainties 24
Chinese Chews.............................121
Chocolate Carousels....................... 31
Chocolate Date Nut Squares 88
Chocolate Fruit Squares 99
Chocolate Peanut Squares 32
Festive Fruit 43
Fruit Marmalade Squares 55
Fruit Roll.. 20
Fruity Fruit Slice 62
Graham Cracker Chew 87
Matrimonial Squares 50
Merry Fruit Bars 97
Mystery Cake 148
Orange Coconut Chews................114
Orange Date Bars 118
Date Pecan Bars 95
Double Brownies 74

Easy Graham Bars 104

Fancy Whip Up 11
Festive Fruit 43
Festive Fruit Cake 67
Five-Cup Slice 78
Flat Truffles 16
Frieda's Number 89 109
Fruit
Bridge Peel Dainties 24

Festive Fruit 43
   Festive Fruit Cake 67
   Merry Fruit Bars 97
Fruit Cocktail Bars 81
Fruit Marmalade Squares 55
Fruit Roll 20
Fruity Fruit Slice 62
Fudgy Macaroons 20

Ginger Bar 122
Ginger Shortbread 49
Graham Cracker Chew 87
Graham Mint Roll 19
Grant's Special 119
Gumdrop Bars 78

Hermit Slice 47
Honey
   Australian Honey Bars 97
   Chocolate Crisps 10
   Poppy Seed Squares 150

Jam
   Banana Bars 66
   Chocolate Nut Shortcake 57
   Fruit Marmalade Squares 55
   Marmalade Bars 102
   Marzipan Bars 73
   Raspberry Bars 94
   Raspberry Meringue 142
   Raspberry Smacks 117
   Sesame Squares 137
Jellied Marshmallows 26

Lemon
   Coconut Lemon Bars 101
   Lemon Crumb Squares 120
   Lemon Crunch 60
   Lemon Graham Slice 130
   Lemon Mardi Gras 139
   Lemon Slice 48
   Lemon Smacks 138
   Lemon Squares 116

Magic Bars 124
Marble Squares 68
Marmalade Bars 102
Marshmallow Roll 38

Marshmallow Squares 46
Marshmallows
   Bridge Peel Dainties 24
   Butterscotch Confetti 33
   Chocolate Confetti 28
   Chocolate Roll 8
   Chocolate TV Roll 28
   Festive Fruit 43
   Jellied Marshmallows 26
   Marble Squares 68
   Nummies 37
   Pineapple Log 39
   Rice Krispies 9
   Saucepan Brownies 23
   S'Mores 10
   TV Roll 32
Marzipan Bars 73
Matrimonial Squares 50
Meringue
   Chocolate Smacks 147
   Grant's Special 119
   Lemon Slice 48
   Lemon Smacks 138
   Nut Smacks 129
   Raspberry Meringue 142
   Raspberry Smacks 117
Merry Fruit Bars 97
Midnight Mints 13
Millionaire Squares 45
Mincemeat Squares 75
Molasses Bars 93
Mystery Cake 148

Nanaimo Bars 40
Neapolitan Squares 83
Nummies 37
Nut Smacks 129
Nutted Gumdrops 112
Nutty Bars 52
Nutty Spice Slice 58

Oh Henry Bars 44
Oh Henry Butterscotch 14
Orange Coconut Chews 114
Orange Date Bars 118
Orange Squares 105
Peanut Butter
   Butterscotch Confetti 28

155

Cereal Slice 15
Chocolate Carousels 31
Chocolate Confetti 28
Chocolate Crisps 10
Chocolate Peanut Squares 32
Coconut Roll 12
Krispy Krunch Bars 38
Peanut Krispie Squares 41
Peanut Butter Bars 82
Peanut Butter Chip Squares 146
Peanut Butter Rice Krispies 9
Peanut Krispie Squares 41
Peanuts
Chocolate Crisps 10
Chocolate Nut Shortcake 57
Five-Cup Slice 78
Grant's Special 119
Peppermint
Chocolate Peppermint Slice 128
Graham Mint Roll 19
Midnight Mints 13
Pineapple
Caribbean Bars 63
Fruit Roll 20
Pineapple Bars 59
Pineapple Brownies 69
Pineapple Filled Bars 104
Pineapple Log 39
Poppy Seed Squares 150
Potato Chip Bars 106
Prune Chips 98
Puffed Wheat Squares 26

Quick Hurry Bars 79

Rainbow Pastel 25
Raisin Quickie 22
Raisin Spice Bars 149
Raisin Squares 103
Raisins
Australian Honey Bars 97
Butter Tart Bars 140
Coconut Lemon Bars 101
Cranberry Squares 113
Festive Fruit 43
Five-Cup Slice 78
Fruit Marmalade Squares 55
Fruit Roll 20
Ginger Bar 122

Hermit Slice 47
Nutty Spice Slice 58
Orange Squares 105
Three Layer Slice 111
Raspberry Bars 94
Raspberry Meringue 142
Raspberry Smacks 117
Rice Krispies 9
Rolled Oats
Banana Oat Squares 49
Chewy Candy Bars 115
Cranberry Oat Squares 56
Gumdrop Bars 78
Matrimonial Squares 50
Mincemeat Squares 75

Saucepan Brownies 23
Scotch Shortbread 56
Sesame Squares 137
Shortbread
Caramel Shortbread 131
Ginger Shortbread 49
Scotch Shortbread 56
S'Mores 10
Snow Log 24
Spice
Almond Bars 151
Apple Squares 70
Cinnamon Bars 132
Festive Fruit 43
Frieda's Number 89 109
Ginger Bar 122
Ginger Shortbread 49
Hermit Slice 47
Molasses Bars 93
Nutty Spice Slice 58
Prune Chips 98
Raisin Spice Bars 149
Swirl Squares 127

Three Layer Slice 111
TV Roll 32
Tropical Treat 29
Tweed Squares 100

Walnut Bars 145

MAIL ORDER FORM

Company's Coming Cookbooks Are Available at Retail Locations Everywhere

Deduct $5.00 for every $35.00 ordered

Save $5.00

COMPANY'S COMING SERIES

ENGLISH

Quantity	Title	Quantity	Title	Quantity	Title
	150 Delicious Squares		Vegetables		Microwave Cooking
	Casseroles		Main Courses		Preserves
	Muffins & More		Pasta		Light Casseroles
	Salads		Cakes		Chicken, Etc.
	Appetizers		Barbecues		Kids Cooking
	Desserts		Dinners of the World		Fish & Seafood (NEW)
	Soups & Sandwiches		Lunches		Breads (NEW)
	Holiday Entertaining		Pies		Meatless Cooking (April 1997)
	Cookies		Light Recipes		

NO. OF BOOKS   PRICE

FIRST BOOK: $12.99 + $3.00 shipping = **$15.99 each** x _____ = $ _____

ADDITIONAL BOOKS: $12.99 + $1.50 shipping = **$14.49 each** x _____ = $ _____

PINT SIZE BOOKS

Quantity	Title	Quantity	Title	Quantity	Title
	Finger Food		Buffets		Chocolate
	Party Planning		Baking Delights		

NO. OF BOOKS   PRICE

FIRST BOOK: $4.99 + $2.00 shipping = **$6.99 each** x _____ = $ _____

ADDITIONAL BOOKS: $4.99 + $1.00 shipping = **$5.99 each** x _____ = $ _____

JEAN PARÉ LIVRES DE CUISINE

FRENCH

Quantity	Titre	Quantity	Titre	Quantity	Titre
	150 délicieux carrés		Délices des fêtes		Les casseroles légères
	Les casseroles		Recettes légères		Poulet, etc.
	Muffins et plus		Les salades		La cuisine pour les enfants
	Les dîners		La cuisson au micro-ondes		Poissons et fruits de mer
	Les barbecues		Les pâtes		Les pains (NEW)
	Les tartes		Les conserves		La cuisine sans viande (avril 1997) (NEW)

NO. OF BOOKS   PRICE

FIRST BOOK: $12.99 + $3.00 shipping = **$15.99 each** x _____ = $ _____

ADDITIONAL BOOKS: $12.99 + $1.50 shipping = **$14.49 each** x _____ = $ _____

TOTAL

- **MAKE CHEQUE OR MONEY ORDER PAYABLE TO:** *COMPANY'S COMING PUBLISHING LIMITED*
- **ORDERS OUTSIDE CANADA:** *Must be paid in U.S. funds by cheque or money order drawn on Canadian or U.S. bank.*
- *Prices subject to change without prior notice.*
- *Sorry, no C.O.D.'s*

TOTAL PRICE FOR ALL BOOKS	$
Less $5.00 for every $35.00 ordered −	$
SUBTOTAL	$
Canadian residents add G.S.T. +	$
TOTAL AMOUNT ENCLOSED	$

Please complete shipping address on reverse.

Gift Giving

- Let us help you with your gift giving!
- We will send cookbooks directly to the recipients of your choice if you give us their names and addresses.
- Be sure to specify the titles you wish to send to each person.
- If you would like to include your personal note or card, we will be pleased to enclose it with your gift order.
- Company's Coming Cookbooks make excellent gifts. Birthdays, bridal showers, Mother's Day, Father's Day, graduation or any occasion... collect them all!

Shipping address

Send the Company's Coming Cookbooks listed on the reverse side of this coupon, to:

Name:

Street:

City: Province/State:

Postal Code/Zip: Tel: (   ) —

Company's Coming Publishing Limited
Box 8037, Station F
Edmonton, Alberta, Canada T6H 4N9
Tel: (403) 450-6223
Fax: (403) 450-1857

Available April 1997

MEATLESS COOKING

New and Imaginative Ways
to cook up meals your family will love!

- Appetizers, Dips
- Casseroles, Stews
- Desserts
- Pasta, Pizza
- Pies, Quiches
- Sandwiches, Burgers
- Soups, Salads
- Vegetables

Mark your favorite recipe with this handy tear out COOKMARK

Company's Coming COOKBOOKS

Quick & Easy Recipes

Everyday Ingredients

OVER 10 MILLION SOLD IN SERIES

Cookmark

Complete your collection.

Look for these *Best-Sellers* where you shop!

COMPANY'S COMING SERIES
Suggested Retail $12.99 each

- ☐ 150 DELICIOUS SQUARES
- ☐ CASSEROLES
- ☐ MUFFINS & MORE
- ☐ SALADS
- ☐ APPETIZERS
- ☐ DESSERTS
- ☐ SOUPS & SANDWICHES
- ☐ HOLIDAY ENTERTAINING
- ☐ COOKIES
- ☐ VEGETABLES
- ☐ MAIN COURSES
- ☐ PASTA
- ☐ CAKES
- ☐ BARBECUES
- ☐ DINNERS OF THE WORLD
- ☐ LUNCHES
- ☐ PIES
- ☐ LIGHT RECIPES
- ☐ MICROWAVE COOKING
- ☐ PRESERVES
- ☐ LIGHT CASSEROLES
- ☐ CHICKEN, ETC.
- ☐ KIDS COOKING
- ☐ FISH & SEAFOOD
- ☐ BREADS
- ☐ MEATLESS COOKING (April 1997)

PINT SIZE BOOKS
Suggested Retail $4.99 each

- ☐ FINGER FOOD
- ☐ PARTY PLANNING
- ☐ BUFFETS
- ☐ BAKING DELIGHTS
- ☐ CHOCOLATE

All New Recipes

Sample Recipe from Meatless Cooking

ZUCCHINI CUTLETS

So colorful with red and green showing throughout. A wonderful addition to a meal.

Finely grated carrot	½ cup	125 mL
Chopped onion	½ cup	125 mL
Chopped red pepper	¼ cup	60 mL
Chopped green pepper	¼ cup	60 mL
Fine soda cracker crumbs	2 cups	500 mL
All-purpose flour	¼ cup	60 mL
Baking powder	1 tsp.	5 mL
Salt	¾ tsp.	4 mL
Pepper	⅛ tsp.	0.5 mL
Grated zucchini, with peel	3 cups	750 mL
Large eggs, lightly beaten	2	2
Cooking oil	2 tbsp.	30 mL

Measure first 9 ingredients into bowl. Stir.

Mix in zucchini and eggs. Shape into cutlets (patties) using about ¼ cup (60 mL) for each.

Heat cooking oil in frying pan. Brown cutlets on both sides. Makes about 1 dozen.

Variation: For more protein add grated cheese.

Use this handy checklist to complete your collection of **Company's Coming Cookbooks**